Odyssey

Dynamic Learning System

A Treasure Trove Book

Odyssey

Dynamic Learning System

A Treasure Trove Book

David Pinto and Leon Conrad

Winchester, UK
Washington, USA

First published by Liberalis Books, 2015
Liberalis Books is an imprint of John Hunt Publishing Ltd., Laurel House, Station Approach,
Alresford, Hants, SO24 9JH, UK
office1@jhpbooks.net
www.liberalisbooks.com

For distributor details and how to order please visit the 'Ordering' section on our website.

Text copyright: David Pinto and Leon Conrad 2014

ISBN: 978 1 78279 296 3

A CIP catalogue record for this book is available from the British Library.

Design: Stuart Davies

Printed and bound by CPI Group (UK) Ltd, Croydon, CR0 4YY

We operate a distinctive and ethical publishing philosophy in all
areas of our business, from our global network of authors to
production and worldwide distribution.

CONTENTS

David elaborates on the importance of social learning, and how the Learning Grid democratises the process by which people choose their learning journey together.

Create your own Odyssey Grid
In which David and Leon suggest ways in which you can create your own version of each type of grid, and in the process, explain how design and delivery are inextricably linked, concluding with an invitation for you to design your own version which they'd love to hear about.

Facilitate an Odyssey journey
In which Leon and David share their thoughts on how to facilitate an Odyssey journey for a group from start to finish, covering the set-up, dynamics, use of questions, manner of choosing activities, the possibility of using colours and shapes as codes for activity types, how to facilitate connections, how to gauge whether an Odyssey journey is going well, and how to find the right state of balance when facilitating.

Using Kagan Structures with groups
In which Leon shares his thoughts on Kagan Structures, how they facilitate productive cooperative learning experiences for journeyers, and why they are ideally suited for use with Odyssey Grids; along with some thoughts about finding the right state of balance between cooperative and collaborative learning styles when facilitating an Odyssey journey.

Variations
In which variations in timing, questioning and journeying are explored, along with variant ways of structuring, constructing and delivering Odyssey Grids; suggestions for varying content are presented, culminating in an invitation to try these systems out in practice for yourself.

Acknowledgements

David Pinto:

First, thanks to the GCSE class at Whitton High School, who responded positively to the **On Yer Bike** maths experiment, showing courage and determination in the face of algebra; thanks to the students of Queen Anne High School, Dunfermline, for your outstanding performance when participating in All-Terrain Math – I was privileged to teach you; thanks to the students at Humphry Davy School, Penzance, for experiencing the world premiere of *Maths Xtreme* with such enthusiasm, enthusing me with confidence; and double thanks to the students and staff at Newbury Hall International School for continuing the Odyssey journey, proving metacognitive skills are cross-cultural. Thanks to Leon for taking an interest in mathematics while on a bus ride, whose warmth and open-mindedness inspire respect and loyalty. Thanks to Mark Humble and his team at the Maths PGCE at St Margaret's College for introducing how group work should be run, experientially. Last, but not least, thanks also to my teachers at Morgan Academy for their solid, Scottish formal education, and my brother and father – for their informal education around the dinner table, and for their priceless lessons in mental gymnastics.

Leon Conrad:

I'd like to thank David Pinto for introducing me to Odyssey Grids; staff at Sebright School, Hackney, London for supporting the Speech, Sense, Style oracy intervention programme of which the Odyssey Grid formed a part, and all the children in the Speech, Sense, Style class there, academic year 2012–2013, for helping develop it; Giles Abbott and Phil McDermott for their participation in early trials of this with adults, and Tanya and Katya, my wife and daughter, for their support throughout this project.

And from both of us:

We'd both like to thank the talented graphic designer and paper sculptor, Peter Dahmen (www.peterdahmen.de – www.popup-karten.de), for his kind permission to adapt his instructions on how to create an optical illusion for **4D** – one of the activities in this book; Teresa Monachino (www.studiomonachino.co.uk) for her advice and suggestions on cover layout, and the entire publishing and marketing team at Liberalis, for the commitment they've shown to the publication and marketing of this, the first book in the Treasure Trove series. In particular, we'd like to thank Stuart Davies for his design work, Elizabeth Radley and Mollie Barker for their help in copy editing the work, Maria Barry for help with marketing and John Hunt for his publishing support.

Two introductions

David's introduction

Writing an introduction is always tricky. As the author, I'm at the end of my journey; and as the reader, you're at the beginning of yours. And here we meet – at the doorway, as it were.

To be honest, in my early years, I'd skip the introduction, and dive into the material straight off; and if you share this enthusiastic characteristic, feel free to start a reader's journey through an Odyssey Grid (page 14 for Leon's, and page 34 for David's).

(page 14 for Leon's, and page 34 for David's)

* * *

I remember visiting New York a few years ago now. Within a few days, I was invited to watch a Japanese Noh play in a derelict garden as the evening and summer faded. I remember the Twin Towers looming above as I rode with a bunch of cyclists over the wooden slats of Brooklyn Bridge, or drinking delicious smoothies on a rooftop on the Lower East Side of Manhattan. Although we experience our life linearly, I'd be hard pressed to remember the exact chronological order of my New York adventures. The same goes for the order of books I read at university, or perhaps even the order of ideas in a book. It all comes down to narrative, and this is something to do with the stories we tell ourselves – how we connect experiences or collate ideas.

An Odyssey Grid provides us with a way of creating a narrative through a conceptual journey. There's no one way through a syllabus, nor through life for that matter. So, instead of a linear structure, with a neat and tidy progression of beginning, middle and end, we present a non-linear structure, with multiple paths through the material. The beginning, middle and end become the linear narrative of specific paths taken by specific participants – their unique journey; *your* unique journey.

The tourist industry provides the best possible service to as many people as possible. Walks and bus rides, with a menu of splendid sights—the Houses of Parliament or the London Eye or Oxford Street in London—but they tend to come packaged and shrink-wrapped, complete with photos, "I saw this", "I did that". Education can take this form too.

We'd like to approach the learning experience in a different way, so the learning material becomes alive. As alive as it was, say, to the pioneering minds of Newton or Einstein, perhaps.

* * *

School worked for me. Whatever the reasons and conditions, I did well, but I did notice that my peers didn't fare so well. So when I returned to school as a teacher, I was genuinely intrigued by what went wrong. I could see why students didn't connect up material from one class to another sequentially, or from one subject to another. Maths processes chopped up into small, bite-sized pieces—easy enough to swallow, spoon-fed—robbed learners of the challenge of discovery – the seemingly endless breadcrumb trail of processes, day after day; the failed attempt at making the subject 'realistic', the areas of carpets, tiles and paint, rather than the celebration of the unutterable excitement of abstraction; the artificial divide between Maths and English, exaggerated by different teacher personalities, all made cross-curricular thinking a no-man's land.

I was lucky enough to participate in a teaching course run by a very progressive practitioner, Mark Humble, where our training day consisted of playing activities just as our students would. I'm a fan of rote learning for some material, to exercise the trust students have in teachers in learning a conceptual process which is beyond their ability to conceive at any one moment – this is how I learned, after all. Now I was given tools to turn learning into a discovery; a social exploration by teammates, a genuinely fresh approach. I had so much fun doing supply/substitute teaching in inner city schools in London, I'd have paid for the experience!

My greatest learning was that learning happens simultaneously. Whether between several people in a room, or within an individual's mind, there are simultaneous processes going on. We'll be covering this in some detail in this book, by showing how algebra can be learned in one lesson, by emphasising the physical and conceptual learning involved in juggling, by describing the conditions that give rise to the '**Aha!**' moment.

Pirsig goes to some length to describe 'Quality' in his book, *Zen and the Art of Motorcycle Maintenance.*[1] My objective was never to *capture* 'Quality', but to *induce* it live in our classes. Pirsig used a motorbike. We use the Odyssey Grid or Learning Grid.

* * *

The central technique we introduce in this book is that of the Learning Grid. Any syllabus or training content can be turned into a set of activities. Rather than present them linearly, we simply contain them as a two-dimensional grid. Participants pick their way through the material, and thus not only explore the syllabus's content, but do so in a unique sequence. The juxtaposition of activities is where the deeper learning occurs, the ability to associate what may appear to be disparate subjects or topics or processes.

Once the ability to associate different material on a Learning Grid becomes exercised in the student's mind, so it becomes easier for them to associate material between subjects and — beyond this — between different aspects of their lives. So whatever they're getting taught at school relates to what they're doing on the Internet between friends, or to what they see on TV – whether news, documentary or entertainment. Every one of us is now capable of producing videos, films, animations, as well as writing and sharing blog posts, stories and books. We can make music, or jam with friends around the world. The Internet has expanded the practice of 'pen friend' to 'co-creators' of so much more than writing.

There's a revolution being conducted in our schools and in our workplaces. The non-linearity of the Internet maps well to our social networking as well as to how our brains network neurons. Will it be contained in our classrooms, in our offices? Or will we be undergoing a societal change so significant that not only our schools and our offices, but our government and law courts, will change? Such questions are well outside the remit of this book... or are they?

We're living in challenging times, that's for sure. It only takes a moment to review the deplorable degradation to our natural environment to realise the seismic shifts to our institutions are but a consequence. How we fare—each of us individually, and all of us collectively—will determine our fate on this planet. It's our collective Odyssey – and I, for one, invite engagement in ways which are enlightening, inspirational and imminently practical.

Leon's introduction

The first time I met David was on the top of a double-decker bus. Sitting across the aisle, I glanced over at the book he was reading. It was something along the lines of The Zen of Maths, if I recall. The title intrigued me. He noticed me glancing at the book. Rather than doing what many London commuters tend to do, in my experience, nowadays—retreat defensively into their personal space—David simply reached out to offer me the book to look through. An interesting conversation ensued, which led to many others. During a conversation about teaching, David mentioned *Educare*, a book he'd written about innovative approaches to holistic learning he'd developed, and had had the privilege of sharing with students in primary and secondary

4

schools during his time as a supply teacher.

The book included a brief description of an Odyssey Grid, which he called *Maths Xtreme*.[2] A while later I found myself planning a 'Speech, Sense, Style' oracy intervention for a school in East London, which was designed to help students improve their oracy and public speaking skills through a combination of storytelling and an integrated approach to teaching grammar, logic and rhetoric. I asked David about the board again and became fascinated by the links between his idea and some powerful story structures I was familiar with. "There's good educational potential in this," I thought. It turns out that in trying it out, I ended up spontaneously developing a variation on it. The students loved it. They loved the surprise element it introduced, they loved making connections between the content, and they loved being the one to choose what would be covered in that lesson. It was a joy to see how it slowly helped draw out social skills, negotiation techniques, and a community spirit. In practice, it worked very much like a story. As it unfolded, it revealed a magic that I hadn't fully appreciated before. Like the best-told stories, which are presented simply, by a powerful storyteller who masters structure and adapts content to the moment of telling, I found the Learning Grid worked best the more I facilitated, and the less I led, or taught. I continued to develop the idea which is presented here, alongside David's original version, and some other variations we've come up with. That's the beauty of this infinitely flexible content-neutral structure. But enough of the background. Let's get to grips with what an Odyssey Grid is; how it works; why we think it works so well; and how you can build one of your own, and use it to help students acquire not just an understanding of subjects, but deep, connected knowledge of them.

As the project developed, the idea also developed of publishing accompanying books containing cultural riddles for educators wanting to engage learners in understanding subject matter across the curriculum – whether teachers at school or parents at home; and general readers wanting to expand their knowledge, and explore particular subjects in more depth, in a fun way. Thus, the Treasure Trove series of books was born, of which this is the first. You'll find more information about other volumes available from Liberalis at the back of this book.

A basic overview of the Odyssey Dynamic Learning System

What is it?

Well, imagine a colourful grid of shapes put up on a wall, each with a clue behind it. You're asked to go on a journey—your own Odyssey—tracing your own path through this grid. Each grid piece has a riddle, a puzzle, a piece of knowledge you have to seek. Your aim is to tie these together, and make sense of them at the end of your journey. What you'll discover is, as yet, unknown. You'll find the treasure by engaging in the treasure hunt, by undertaking the journey, by going on your own Odyssey. And you'll have loads of fun and surprises on the way.

The Odyssey Grid and the related Treasure Trove series of books aim to engage participants by drawing them into a fun series of mysteries and riddles they have to solve, widening their knowledge of subject matter, and their exposure to shared heritage and cultural references.

Together, they form a visual springboard for developing wisdom through a process of co-discovery and collaborative learning.

Unlike conventional puzzle books, or compendia—which mostly contain puzzles or riddles in linear, closed forms, complete in themselves—Odyssey journeys are non-linear; have a deeper structure; and encourage participants to draw on deep levels of knowledge and awareness in order to reach goals—goals which are typically open-ended, and often defined in terms of destination, but not in terms of the final insight that will be realised once that destination is reached. It's up to individual participants to find those insights for themselves. While the grids in this book are printed in greyscale, colour versions are available on line at www.odysseygrids.com.

What are the benefits?

No two Odyssey journeys are ever the same. Each Odyssey journey has an element of randomness built into it. Each Odyssey journey is an invitation to engage in deep thinking and have fun. The benefits partly depend on the content, and partly on the journey.

Whether building, facilitating or participating in an Odyssey journey, you'll be making new connections in your brain, improving your brainpower, developing your creativity, going on a voyage of self-exploration, expanding your awareness, and potentially increasing your capacity for wisdom. All these things can improve your enjoyment of life, and your experience of being alive.

Best of all, it's not a high-cost, low-value educational intervention. The journey's more about process than product. The value of an Odyssey journey is made manifest through content and delivery.

While you can populate the grid with ideas from the Treasure Trove series, you can equally invest some time and mental effort, and come up with your own content. And you can create your own Odyssey Grid simply and easily with some brightly coloured paper and a set of coloured pens that will allow what you write to show up clearly against these, or use the templates we've designed, available on line.[3]

Who's it for?

Odyssey Grids are suitable for use in schools, in businesses, and with community and learning groups. Individuals can enjoy going on an Odyssey journey in the comfort of their living room, or when commuting or on a long-distance journey. Odyssey Grids can be used by school teachers in primary and secondary settings, by lecturers in colleges and higher education, and by workshop facilitators in business. They're suitable for anyone aged seven upwards.

What are its applications?

The Learning Grid emerged in the context of education. It was originally conceived as an introduction to mathematics: *Maths Xtreme*, where everything was considered mathematics – the ability to notice patterns, and formalise them.

It's a flexible, content-free structure with inherently powerful qualities that allow it to work well in any learning environment. We give examples of applications to schools and business within the book; but you could design one, and put it up on a family living room wall as an alternative to a television set, with each family member contributing a set of activities for a journey the whole family could go on together; or you could design an individual Odyssey Grid as a present for a loved one, so they can take an Odyssey journey you've designed specially for them.

Odyssey Grids in schools

The application to curricula in standard school environments is obvious. We've provided the Algebra Grid in this book as a taster. Subsequent publications in the Treasure Trove series provide activities for specific subjects which can be adapted for various levels and age groups.[4]

Odyssey Grids in businesses

The approach is also highly relevant to corporate training courses and workshops.

Odyssey Grids are well placed in that they emphasise diversity while exercising unity – a sweet spot of social self-organisation. There's a balance between allowing employees to take their own path, and enabling enough social cohesion for the company to progress as a community.

Because of the influence of practices born from the Internet, peer-to-peer networking is becoming standard in business – from crowd-funded start-ups to major corporation intrapreneurs. The traditional chain of command familiar to hierarchical structures—which lends itself well to one-to-many lectures and linear learning—is being complemented by robust social networks, inviting many-to-many engagement, and non-linear learning.

The Learning Grid stands as an experiential micro-example of the path the company is taking in the marketplace, encouraging employees to reflect upon—and comment on—the relationship between different elements of the company and the marketplace, and influence the future direction of a subdivision or the company as a whole. A group of employees could even be encouraged to devise a grid collaboratively, and share it with their peers. Each grid could become a piece in a larger grid, that in turn becomes a piece in a global grid, representing the varied, yet unified whole of a multinational corporation, or even the complex and fascinating activities that are involved in creating any organisation – particularly one with several branches locally, regionally, or nationally.

Because of the underlying philosophy—described by Leon in his section—the Learning Grid enables educators to bring out a finer quality of the learning process. David emphasises the social learning aspect, but this also brings out a sensitivity to learning itself – what we might call metacognitive skills. This is very much the direction mainstream education is going, with cross-curricular activities and project-based courses. Several books in the Treasure Trove series address this directly, providing innovative books of cultural riddles and activities to encourage a sensitivity to thinking alone.

An invitation

At this point, we'd like to invite you to jump in and go on an Odyssey journey with us, or dip your toe in the water of theory and find out more about how they work.

If you're in an activist mood, you can either choose Leon's version, which starts on page 14, or David's, which starts on page 34.

If you're drawn more to investigating theory right now, turn to the theory sections which follow each individual version. For Leon's, see page 23; for David's, page 46.

Practical versions

Leon's version

A treasure revealed

Picture this...

Imagine you're in a room, looking at a colourful grid of many different shapes spread out on a wall. There's something intriguing about it – something almost magical. There are triangles, circles, squares, stars. Each has something on it – a word or diagram. There's one shape of each colour... placed in a strange formation... what could the underlying pattern be? It's as if each shape is a door or a window to another world. It looks like a chocolate box for the mind, or a magical carriage to take you on a journey through your imagination.

Get ready to embark on your very own Odyssey.

It won't be like any journey you've ever gone on before.

Want to find out more? Read on!

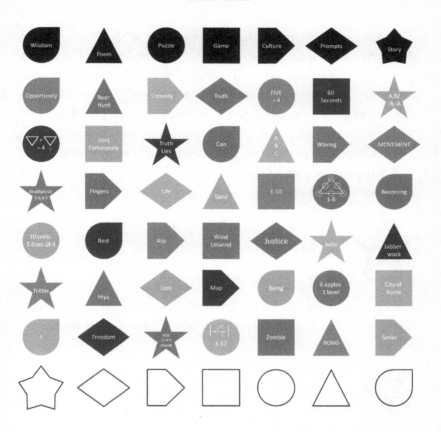

Welcome to the wonderful world of the Odyssey Grid. My version has three distinct sections: a top row with black shapes, a multicoloured grid in the middle, and a bottom row with white shapes.

Look at the top row:

This row contains one example of each shape used in the grid. All the shapes in this row are black. Each shape has a heading word in it. I call it the 'Heading Row'. It provides a key that tells you which category relates to each shape.

In the next section, the shapes in the Heading Row reappear in different colours, arranged randomly across a grid of six rows and seven columns. If you look closely, you'll see they're arranged rather like a Sudoku puzzle, with as little similarity in shape and colour between neighbouring pieces as possible.

In my version, colours are used simply as navigation devices. They don't relate directly to the content of the grid pieces.

Each piece has an intriguing word or diagram on it. Look at this one, for example:

Take a look at the star in the Header Row. This happens to have 'Story' written on it. A story about 'Juice'? What's that about?

And what about this?

Take a look at the teardrop in the Header Row. This happens to have Wisdom written on it. Best wisdom? What's that?

And what's that row of shapes at the bottom?

I call it the Destination Row. It contains the same shapes as in the top row, but they're blank, and in a different order. Why?

The only way to find out is to embark on an Odyssey journey – right now. Once you've tried it on your own, try going on an Odyssey journey with a friend, or in a group. Once you've done that, you'll be ready to facilitate an Odyssey journey for others.

Go on an Odyssey with Leon

Take a look at this Odyssey Grid:

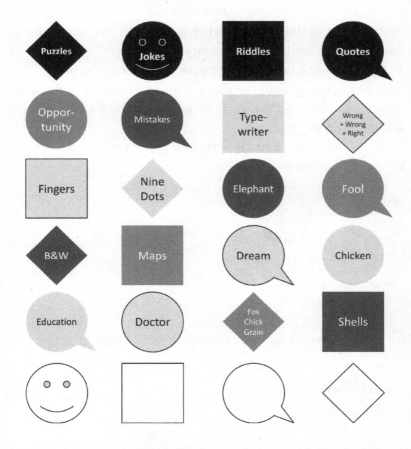

The black Heading Row indicates what each shape stands for, and is used for reference only.

The aim of this journey is to work through the grid, and end up on one of the blank shapes at the bottom in a set number of moves (in this case, you decide how many), to reach a jewel of discovery, as yet unknown. The unknown quality of this goal is what makes an Odyssey journey so exciting. We'll reach it by ultimately linking the experiences of the entire journey back to the category to which the chosen destination shape belongs.

How does it work?

Always start at the top left corner of the grid. (In this example, the blue circle marked **Opportunity**.)

You can move to an adjacent grid piece vertically, or horizontally, but not diagonally; or you can move to a piece of the same colour anywhere on the grid, or to a piece of the same shape anywhere on the grid.

So, in this grid, from **Opportunity** at the top left, you can go to any of these pieces:

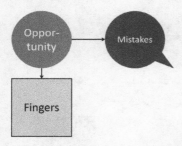

by moving vertically, or horizontally, one shape at a time, or

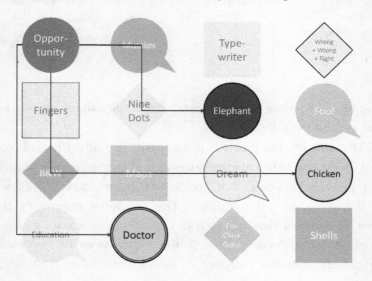

by jumping to a piece of the same shape anywhere on the grid, or

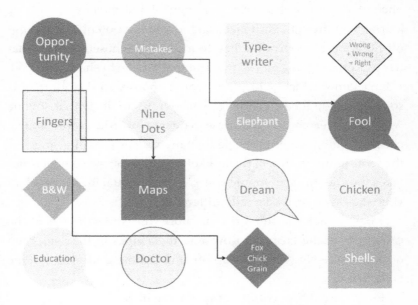

by jumping to a piece of the same colour anywhere on the grid.

Choose the number of stops you want to make on this particular Odyssey. I suggest you choose a number between four and eight stops before you reach your final destination. Make a note of the number of stops you want to take here:

I've decided to take an Odyssey journey using the following number of moves:

Start at the top left piece:

This is an opportunity for you to take an Odyssey journey into uncharted waters. The grid is a map of the territory you'll be journeying through. Each piece on the grid is a potential stopping-off point on the journey, a key to a specially-chosen activity that has personal significance to me, and that I'd like to share with you. I don't know which grid pieces you'll choose, so this journey is something you'll be creating for yourself. It's unlikely that anyone will have ever chosen the same sequence of grid pieces you've chosen before, and improbable that anyone has or will ever go on the same journey – for, in the unlikely event the steps someone else takes through the grid mimic yours, the individual insights each of you takes away will be totally different.

Take a look at the grid. Explore the links between the categories in the Heading Row, and the shapes in the grid; then decide where you want to stop off, and list the grid pieces in the table below.

From here (**Opportunity**), my stops will be:

1.	2.	3.	4.
5.	6.	7.	8.

Now look up each activity in your list in the alphabetical Activities Section at the back of the book, tackling them in order. Complete an activity, and reflect on what you've learned. As you progress, note the connections you discover for yourself between the activities.

Use the following boxes to make notes as you go:

1. What I learned was:

2. What I learned was:

How it connected to my previous learning point.

3. What I learned was:

How it connected to my previous learning points.

4. What I learned was:

How it connected to my previous learning points.

5. What I learned was:

How it connected to my previous learning points.

6. What I learned was:

How it connected to my previous learning points.

7. What I learned was:

How it connected to my previous learning points.

8. What I learned was:

How it connected to my previous learning points.

Using the rules of navigation (jump to a piece directly below, or of the same shape as the one you're on), you now get to choose your destination:

| Jokes | Riddles | Quotations | Puzzles |

Look up your chosen destination point in the Activities Section at the back. Note the culmination of your learning here:

What's the thinking behind it?

There are four essential components to this Odyssey Grid:

- a Header Row of shapes at the top;
- a Destination Row of shapes at the bottom;

- a grid of coloured shapes between these rows;
- a starting point, always to be found below the top left header shape.

Each serves a particular purpose.

The Header Row

This is the key to this version of the Odyssey Grid. Each shape in this row denotes a category. Every piece in the Odyssey Grid that matches one of these shapes will fit into the category shown in the Header Row. In this row, the shapes are different, but the colour's constant. The Header Row colour isn't repeated anywhere else in the grid.

It provides a constant point of reference for the categories that the different shapes generically fit under.

The Destination Row

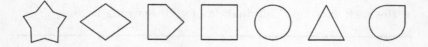

The goal of this version of the Odyssey journey is always to end up on one of the shapes in this row. These match the shapes that appear in the Header Row, but there's a difference. The shapes in the Destination Row are blank.

The Destination Row provides an array of possible destinations, each relating to one of the categories featured in the Header Row. The shapes in the Destination Row are blank because the content of the destination is as yet unknown. The undefined quality of the destination adds to the intrigue and excitement of the journey, as the mysterious jewel at the heart of the final destination only emerges from the act of synthesising the connections made as a result of journeying through the grid.

The grid

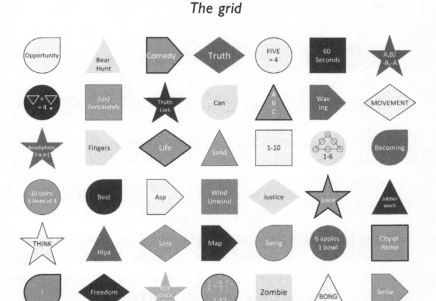

The grid's made up of a number of different coloured shapes. There are as many shapes as there are columns, and as many multiples of each shape as there are rows.

Header Row							
1	1	2	3	4	5	6	7
2							
3							
4			(7 x 6 = 42 pieces)				
5							
6							
Destination Row							

Within the basic framework of the fixed elements of Header Row, grid, Destination Row and starting point, Odyssey Grids are extremely—almost infinitely—adaptable structures. You can adapt:

- size,
- shapes,
- colours,
- content.

You can also explore many variations in terms of interaction, structure, construction, timing, and much more – see the Variations Section (page 70).

The starting point

In both David's version of the Odyssey Grid and mine, the starting piece is consistently the top left piece of the grid. We recommend keeping this a constant feature. After all, you have to start somewhere. We chose top rather than bottom to fit with the analogy of 'drilling down' to find a rich core of knowledge. It also seemed more fun to start at the top, rather than the bottom. If you feel very strongly about doing it differently, go right ahead – change the pattern to suit your temperament when you design your own!

How does it work at a meta level?
The display

Traditional static educational displays (as opposed to displays of students' work) tend to be content-rich, colourful visual renditions of topics or information that students are *required* to learn, presented beautifully, but at face value. Factual interactive whiteboard displays are often no different. Both typically present the visual equivalent of statements, rather than questions. Both are the visual instructional equivalent of the old-fashioned 'jug-mug' approach to teaching.[5] Neither is structured to invite students to make new connections. I don't know of a single teacher who's ever asked students to connect the content of one display to another.

Having an Odyssey Grid up on a wall transforms a classroom into an alchemical alembic for interactive, cooperative education. Like the walls and floors of medieval cathedrals such as that of Chartres in France, richly decorated with symbolic forms such as rose windows or labyrinths, the history of which reaches back thousands of years[6]—or like the 'vaulted books' of buildings such as that of the so-called Spanish Chapel adjoining the Basilica of Santa Maria Novella in Florence[7]—Odyssey Grids invite participants to go on a structured journey that takes them way past the two-dimensional network on display. Just as programmatic images and geometric windows once served as icons that acted as boundaries between symbol and symbolic, content-sparse Odyssey Grids entice participants to go beyond the initial prompt given on each grid piece, inviting deep-level interaction. While neither a maze, nor a labyrinth, the open-ended choice of pathway that an Odyssey journey offers encourages participants to enter a similar experience to that which they'd get if navigating a maze or a labyrinth. At each step, a new vista opens, and new horizons appear. The arrival at the destination provides an opportunity to reflect on the path taken, and retrace it to make sense of the connections, and see the starting position in a new light – the light of revelation.

The display itself; the riddle-like quality of the pieces, with their enigmatic one-word or sketched-out invitations; the open-ended, riddle-like structure I recommend the content behind them having are all ideally suited to developing deep thinking. The visual shorthand used here acts like visual acupuncture on the mind. The display encourages journeyers to enter into the essence of a symbol; rather than remain on the surface of the grid, simply studying the symbols themselves.

The open-ended, riddle-like qualities of each piece in both the grid and Destination Row are designed to awaken curiosity and encourage a search for meaning. This is a powerful way to encourage learning – particularly if this search results in a quantum leap in understanding. An Odyssey journey is ideally suited to making this happen.

Research has shown that recognising similarities and differences, and using metaphors and analogies, are some of the best ways to encourage deep thought and understanding.[8] The unstated connection between grid pieces and Header Row categories invites journeyers to actively explore the possible connections. Working collaboratively, with personal accountability, they typically come up with several possible solutions. When this creative approach to flexible thinking is allowed to flourish by the facilitator, it can have a profound effect.

In addition, every Odyssey journey, every piece that makes up an Odyssey Grid has maieutic potential. The maieutic potential of an Odyssey journey can be brought to the fore by facilitators who use questions to bring forth responses from participators. The word maieutic is associated with Socratic dialogue, and is related to the Greek word for midwifery. It describes a method for the awakening of participants to insights related to experiences that may be latent within them, but that they may not have brought into their conscious thinking, or to create links between existing knowledge, values, and new information. For more information on maieutic questioning, see page 71.

Random connections force participants to interrogate unusual or unconventional relationships. Particular types of interactions—such as the Unending Line of Questioning variation (see page 72)—bring this type of thinking to the fore.

The journey

American storyteller Kendall Haven was once challenged by senior stakeholders at NASA. He claimed they'd be more effective in getting people to understand important information by using stories than if they tried to use a more formal style in their outreach programmes. The then director said, "Prove it." Haven subsequently trawled through over 350 research studies in 15 fields, and concluded in his book, *Story Proof*, that *any curriculum information will be learned better and more effectively if presented within the context of story structure.*[9]

Odyssey journeys share the same structure as many traditional stories. When you go on an Odyssey journey, you're intrinsically following a traditional 6-part story structure, which is hard-wired in us. It's a structure we use to solve problems, to make sense of our experiences.

Let's compare Red Riding Hood's journey to an Odyssey journey:

Story structure	Red Riding Hood's journey	Odyssey journey
1 – Introduction	Once upon a time	The Odyssey Grid offers a doorway to an unusual experience
2 – Characters, setting, and problem	Red Riding Hood, mother, and grandmother introduced	The rules of the grid are introduced
3 – Journey	Red Riding Hood sets off through the forest	The Odyssey journey starts
4 – Enemy/hindrance	She meets the wolf, who eats her grandmother and her	Challenges of finding solutions to dichotomous problems are raised
5 – Friend/helper	The woodcutter comes to the rescue	Solutions and resolutions are found
6 – Outcome	He rescues Red Riding Hood and the grandmother	The Destination Row is reached
7 – Conclusion	And everyone lives happily ever after	Looped links are made, and the resulting understanding is brought forward into the conscious mind

The structure given here is an individual variation on Mooli Lahad's 6-part story structure.[10] This choice deliberately acknowledges the fact that components do not always come—or need to come—in the order Lahad gives (stages 4 and 5 are reversed here, compared to Lahad's model).[11] Within a complex story, there can be many iterations of stages 3–6 before the final outcome that leads to the conclusion. Jack and the Beanstalk is an example, where Jack climbs the beanstalk three times before the final outcome and conclusion are reached.[12] This feature maps precisely the flexibility of the Odyssey journey, where every turn taken within the grid is a new iteration of these stages.

The individual variation on Lahad's 6-part story structure used above also acknowledges the importance of framing a story – the ritualistic 'once upon a time' and 'they lived happily ever after' statements that invoke and delineate thresholds for entry into and return from the story world. The qualitative difference of entering the story world often manifests as a state of being transported into a state of 'flow'.[13] We observed that students show the same traits when engaging with an Odyssey journey as when engaged in a storytelling performance. Because the content is open-ended, there's a good match between skill level and challenge. The riddle quality of the grid pieces makes engagement interesting, without being too challenging. We've noted that journeyers really enjoy the experience of having a problem 'get under their skin', sometimes living with it for the span of a few days, trying to work it out. When a facilitator allows this state to continue—while supporting and encouraging journeyers to find their own solutions, in order to bring them back to the group, and share them together—then deep transformational learning can happen.

An Odyssey journey's also similar to a structure used in gamestorming[14] – a problem-solving approach devised by a team at XPLANE, a graphic design company in Portland, Oregon, USA, founded by Dave Gray. Their innovative, highly visual techniques allow groups to work together to arrive at a commonly devised solution or goal. While timescales for gamestorming activities and Odyssey journeys may differ, both share features of the story structure variation outlined above. Like a gamestorming session, an Odyssey journey highlights opening (divergent), exploring (emergent) and closing (convergent) stages. It also shares all ten elements of a successful gamestorming session:

- Opening and Closing: the binary form that breathes life into a process.
  - An Odyssey journey has clearly defined opening and closing points, on both whole-grid and individual-piece levels. At the whole-grid level, the fixed 'Opportunity' piece as starting point, and the final Destination Row piece as landing point for the Odyssey journey are clear opening and closing elements. At the individual-piece level, while the grid will have been surveyed, and the intriguing prompts wondered about, there is always an initial act of choice that results in journeyers landing on a piece. This opens up the possibility for an exploratory encounter. Once the content's resolved, there's a sense of closure before the process is repeated once more with a new grid piece, until the journey's finally resolved when the final destination's reached.
- Fire Starting: techniques that light up the imagination and initiate a quest or search.
  - An Odyssey Grid offers a structured, open-ended visual impetus for a learning quest that gives a safe framework within which pathways of exploration can be pursued, maximising the opportunity for enlightenment through the use of open-ended content.
- Artifacts: playing pieces which have the potential to contain a rich set of information.
  - An Odyssey journey's based on a visual array of pieces which act as navigational guides throughout the journey. Any exploration of the ideas behind them can be enriched through use of external props and materials, and used as a rich, varied, but purely mental process of exploration. The latter approach works better with older children or adults who are capable of—and interested in—exploring abstract thought

31

patterns and thinking per se.

- Node Generation: making a generic whole out of individual parts.
  - The structure of an Odyssey journey is based on selecting and linking particular nodes on a given grid.
- Meaningful Space: a way of creating boundaries for a world that can then be explored and mapped creatively.
  - The essential components of any Odyssey Grid—Header Row, Destination Row, grid, and starting point—have this function.
- Sketching and Model Making: using pictures, diagrams and visual language to symbolise complex concepts.
  - Beyond the use of differently-shaped pieces of the grid, which—apart from the Destination Row—typically feature a single-word prompt, or quick sketch, Odyssey journeys offer a content-free opportunity to explore concepts separately, and in relationship to each other; individually, and in groups, using a wide range of means appropriate to the context in which the Odyssey journey is being explored. Multi-sensory exploration just adds to the fun.
- Randomness, Reversal, and Reframing: ways of tricking the mind into finding new solutions to problems, new connections to ideas.
  - Randomness is built into the structure of any Odyssey journey. When the Destination Row is reached, the connections have to be made through a process of reversal, which encourages new thought-links to be formed; reshaping discoveries and tacit knowledge into new, consciously-constructed, connected modes of thought.
- Improvisation: responding intuitively and creating in the moment.
  - The ability to improvise in terms of moving from one

grid piece to another during the creative exploratory (emergent) phase is built into the very structure of every Odyssey journey. The improvisatory quality is highlighted in the Questioning variations and the Random Odyssey Journey (pages 71 and 78 respectively).

- Selection: distilling an open-ended process into manageable chunks to arrive at a focused output.
  - Selection is part of any Odyssey journey, the number of stopping points within the grid being limited by the time available, and the context in which the journey's being taken. The closing (convergent) stage is limited to a choice of a single piece in the Destination Row, which is associated with a category in the Header Row. Not only does this tie the process together, it also gives focus to the meaningful exploration of the links between the grid elements touched on, the final selection, and the resulting generation of content.
- Try Something New: being innovative, being in the present.
  - Novelty and the element of surprise feature in every Odyssey journey. When journeying in groups, individuals and teams can provide different insights and approaches which a skilful facilitator can bring forth to ensure novelty and fun are kept at the heart of the exploratory process.

David's version

Odyssey

If the following were a map, could you find where you are right now?

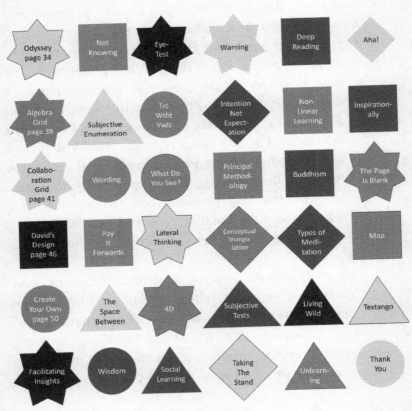

You're in the **Odyssey** part of this book, which is represented in the grid above by the star at the top left. It has a page reference on it which coincides with the beginning of this section. Each coloured shape represents a section of writing or sample activity.

In my version of the Learning Grid, the content is arranged in columns. In this one, the left-hand column represents a linear journey you can take through this book, with each section marked with the number of the page on which it starts. Alternatively, you can choose any of the activities in the top row, and work your way down gradually. Where no page numbers are given, the activity descriptions will be found in the Activities Section at the back of the book where they're arranged alphabetically.

So, at this moment in time, you can choose to move to **Algebra Grid**, or any of the other coloured shapes in the top row – **Not Knowing, Eye-Test, Warning, Deep Reading**, or **Aha!**

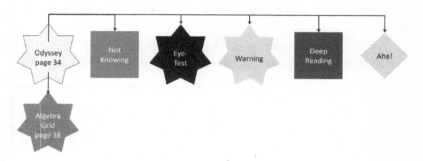

Let's say you choose **Eye-Test** next. Once you've completed that activity, you can then continue with **Algebra Grid, Not Knowing, Txt Wtht Vwls, Warning, Deep Reading**, or **Aha!** as shown below.

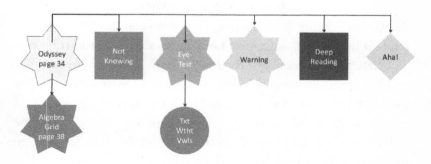

In this way, I invite you to make your way down the grid, one activity at a time, careful not to skip activities as you deepen your journey into the grid.

Your choice, your journey.

If you're going to jump around, my advice is to check out the **Warning** activity first. The nature of this journey is to learn by doing! I want us to push the boundaries of what's possible in terms of the reader-writer experience, which is—after all—the only social dimension we have available here in a book.

So here you are, still in the **Odyssey** section. Where do you want to go? Straight down the left-hand column or jump around?

Which appeals to you? To read linearly as the material is presented in the book sequence, or to go off the beaten trail, and explore non-linearly?

What did you decide and why?

Make a note of your answer here.

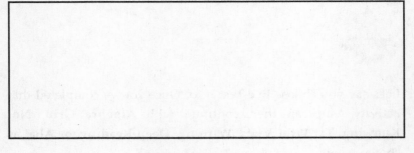

A few words of advice

Please give yourself a few minutes between activities. Try to relate it to previous activities. Let your mind relax, and trust that associations will arise. Put the book down, and contemplate.

I know this is difficult. Whenever I've read instructions to 'put the book down', or faced empty boxes to fill with my answer, I never have. Until—that is—I overcame my respect for the published page, and began writing notes in the margins, and on the blank pages at the back. So, I've put in a few blank pages at the back of the book – feel free to use them to make notes.

After the next activity, please put the book down, close your eyes, and consider for a moment not only each activity, but the relation between them. After a reading session of four or five activities, many associations will come to mind – as well as the potential of a genuine, singular '**Aha!**' moment.

This gem-of-a-moment is what the Odyssey journey's about. So, if you write one thing in this book, let it be something about your first, genuine, insightful thought, so the next reader can read about what arose for you *between* reading—and doing—the activities.

Algebra Grid

The Odyssey Grid in education

Leon and I have intimated that the structure of a Learning Grid provides learners with a non-linear path through a syllabus or course. This can be used quite generally, eg to improve creativity or thinking skills, but it can also be used very precisely to teach specific mental processes. Let's look at algebra.

What we're about to see shouldn't be that surprising. We've all faced algebra—or the teaching of algebra—at some time in our lives. Some people pick it up immediately; most take longer; and quite a few have such difficulty with it, they carry their school experience with them all their lives. I know many people falter, stumble, and—indeed—fall at the first hurdles. Most people— and indeed, teachers—put it down to ability or aptitude at mathematics. I put it down to our manner of teaching it.

Most mathematics is taught linearly, which fits the format of a textbook, one page at a time. Most students are willing to trust the teacher, and learn some process, eg $2x + 3x = 5x$, and do an exercise. Then they're given another process, eg $3(x + 2) = 3x + 6$, another exercise, another process, another exercise. At some point, if these processes tie together, and the connections make sense, the purpose of learning these processes becomes clear; an internal sense of understanding emerges beyond trusting the teacher, and being a dutiful student. Then we have a happy student. Many students end up doing many exercises, and learning processes without really understanding what they're doing – and when things get more complex, they don't have the plasticity of thinking to adapt.

And it gets worse. Those students who don't get it are tortured for years, with the same material being presented to them, year after year, in smaller and more nonsensical 'bite-sized' chunks. So many teenagers are spoon-fed algebra like they're babies. It's an insult to them, and to the professionals who are forced to do it.

No wonder many adolescents resent it. Why are they being treated as stupid at sixteen years of age when they simply didn't get what was taught them when they were eleven? Brain development goes a long way in those years, and sadly the scarification of a bad learning experience can be allowed to last a lifetime.

Even before I qualified as a maths teacher, as a trainee teacher, I hit upon a way of teaching algebra that seemed to work. I used what later came to be named as **Simultaneous Processes** (which you can find on the Collaboration Grid), which was one of the seed ideas for the Learning Grid itself.

Example 4x3 Algebra Grid

There are various ways the grid could be designed. Here's a simple 4x3 Learning Grid, with activities described in the Activities Section at the back of this book, as an example of how an Odyssey Grid can be used in an educational context:

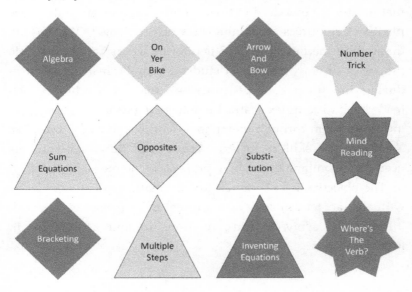

The Algebra Grid could have been preceded by a Fraction Grid, or by a more extensive Arithmetic Grid. In addition, if we created a 5x5 Algebra Grid, we might've had a column including coordinates, plotting points on a line, the equation of the line, intersections, and curved lines, or included a row which introduces the notion of unknowns or variables. The grid could be further expanded into other branches of mathematics. Theoretically, a whole syllabus could be represented in this way – but this would be defeating the point unless the facilitator of the journey creates their own grid, outlining their individual approach to the teaching of the syllabus, so that the design—and the learning—are personalised.

What determines the size of the grid is the time available to journey through it, and how much of a stretch it may be for the learners. A sense of completion is important, and tackling a 3x3 grid is much more comprehensible to a young mind; a large 10x10 grid can be very intimidating. Consider the size as the stretch of sea to be crossed, or the mountain to be climbed.

I've only given a gist of the kind of mathematical operations that need to be practised in the Activities Section, since there are plenty of resources containing lists of problems.[15] What we're doing with the Learning Grid is offering a way for these subtle processes to be combined in students' minds. Instead of introducing the three concepts/processes/rules of algebra (which lends itself to complex abstract language that is unnecessary), we introduce them through metaphors (learning to ride a bike: **On Yer Bike**; and skill at archery: **Arrow And Bow**). All students need do is combine these three processes – no more, no less.

The objective isn't so much to map mathematical knowledge with abstract terminology as to present three processes in a two-dimensional array, inviting relationship and association in learners' minds.

Collaboration Grid

The Odyssey Grid in business

The market's evolving. Competition's giving way to collaboration. Wikipedia, MOOCs, and the bitcoin currency are just three such examples. I believe an ecological economics will emerge. I've included the Collaboration Grid as an example of the kind of course that can help a company help its employees embrace innovative collaborative social practices in the workplace.

Imagine this workshop on collaboration

Attendees arrive, register, are given an 'info pack', and are directed to the room where the workshop is to take place.

The room's comfortable, with baroque music playing in the background, perhaps; and coffee and tea available. There's a large grid of coloured shapes on one wall, some whiteboard paper, pens attached by string, desks with Post-it notes, coloured pens—the usual resources—as well as an assortment of objects like juggling balls, Mickey Mouse hands, gyroscopes. Do any of the attendees play around with these? (The facilitators arrive with the participants, pretending to be attendees, so that they get a real sense of what the experience is like, as well as fulfilling their role as guides later (see **Scouting**).)

Several quotes are strewn around the walls, and this might spark some discussion between participants. One poster has the phrase, 'Was it a rat I saw?' Another has the 'Rules for playing Thought Experiments'. The most prominent states, 'We win if we are all seated, quiet and ready by 9am exactly'.

Placed at the front of a bank of chairs is a single chair with an envelope upon which is written: 'Explanation – do this activity first'.

What will the participants do? Will they cotton on? Will they get themselves ready for 9am? Will they mill about until someone begins to ask questions? Will they go back to the registration desk and ask? When 9am hits and no facilitators arrive, will they have enough gumption to open the envelope and conduct the first activity, or will they sit and wait expectantly? How exciting!

* * *

Let's say they're waiting expectantly. A facilitator jumps up from the crowd, congratulates them on their efforts, and introduces themselves a little to assure people they're in the right place. They step over to the envelope, and read the instructions for the activity — **Explanation** — which explains the prominent Learning Grid of coloured shapes on one wall.

> There's a wall with coloured shapes with words on them. This is called the Collaboration Grid. Each shape's an activity. The activities are sorted by colour and shape, and once you do a few, you may start to guess what the categories are. The activities at the bottom are the most interesting, significant and challenging concepts and practices the designer knows. You choose any of the activities at the top, and work your way down, but don't drill all the way down one column – choose broadly, and you'll be better equipped to appreciate what's down there.
>
> Because you're choosing the activities, a new combination or juxtaposition of activities may spark a new idea — either in you or, indeed, the facilitator — and this is what makes the Learning Grid a potentially vital, organic, and insightful tool.
>
> Any questions? Hopefully someone amongst you has the answers. So go ahead – pick your first (proper) activity!

If these instructions are insufficient in any way for people who've read these instructions themselves, at this point the facilitators may have to abandon their **Scouting** role in order to clarify or allay anxieties. They may have to be more appeasing because some participants won't have enjoyed the lack of an established authority figure.

> *Forgive our little deception. As facilitators, we wanted to experience what it was like to be participants, as well as get a sense of what the group does.*
>
> *May I introduce myself a little more, by suggesting that I have alternative ways of doing many things. This Collaboration Grid is a non-linear tool to share insight. If we look around the room, I suspect there are many different learning styles and personalities in the room. And since you're the most valuable resources here, I'd like to access your wisdom!*
>
> *As described — and I can personally validate — what's important as we go through these activities is the journey, the unique combination of activities which may just spark innovation, insight, and even inspiration. But this depends very much on us, and how attentive we are to our own minds, and — more importantly — to one another. I look forward to what we discover!*

Collaboration Learning Grid

This is an example of how a Learning Grid can be introduced. The Learning Grid can be modified or designed from scratch for different audiences by selecting different activities. This one's tailored for collaboration for business folk. The Collaboration Grid can be used 'straight off the wall' as it were, though the facilitator-guides have the choice of making themselves known from the start! (**Scouting** explains why the guides have infiltrated the attendees secretly, like invisible theatre actors, to actively collaborate, if a little bit of mischief isn't reason enough...)

Collaboration Grid

The attendees are faced with their first Learning Grid:

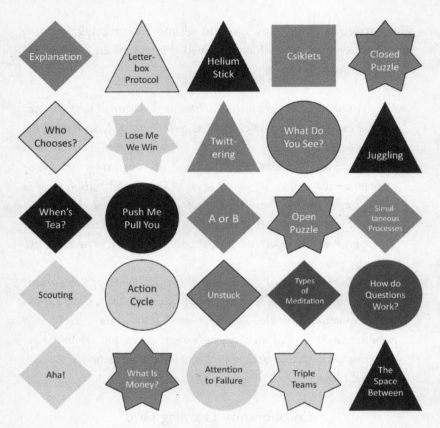

They're free to choose any activity. Perhaps they start with **Who Chooses?** to help the attendees take that first step of collaborative self-determination.

Perhaps someone wants to know what they're going to do that day, what the schedule is – the facilitator can suggest one of the activities, **When's Tea?**.

After a little prompting, all groups understand that everything that's done in the workshop is conducted through the Learning Grid. The facilitator may say something like:

There are loads of resources and activities. I'd love to share them all, but this isn't going to be a normal, linear presentation. Hopefully it's going to be useful, interesting, even deep, maybe even inspira-

tional, but this depends very much on how we gel. What's
important is that the group gets round to accessing as much from
ourselves as possible. Jump in – don't leave it too late in the day...

So the morning continues, with participants calling out the sequence of activities, some of which are games, others a video, others a physical activity, another a bit of theory, another an explanation, another an evaluative exercise, another a break. Each lasts from five to thirty minutes, and participants get the idea that the more they throw themselves into the experience, the stronger the social bonding, the deeper their learning.

The two core activities are **Twittering**, where the participants are encouraged to record their experiences through a series of tweets, and the **Action Cycle**. The facilitator may need to guide the team to these.

Because the index doesn't specify content exactly, the facilitator can determine the content as it follows the continuity of exploration. One activity may be substituted with another similar one if it 'fits' better. What matters is that the group covers a wide range of material.

If the participants use the most valuable resources at their disposal—the people in the room—they'll have unlocked genuine creativity. This is the nature of collaboration, if it's realised!

David's design

The social dimension of a Learning Grid

Whatever the activities, they're only doors which lead participants to a subjective experience. Much of the unique magic of an Odyssey journey lies in how the participants respond to the activities—and to one another as individuals—while journeying. There's an implicit parallel relationship between the activities, and their juxtaposition; between the participants, and their social togetherness.

Obviously the activities are designed to attract attention, but we've already indicated that what's more important is the combination of activities – the unique juxtaposition of activities that have never been brought together before. It's a subtle point which can often be lost if this element's ignored. Participants need to take time to consider the combination of activities – how one follows another, or how three or four fit together during a session. Facilitators need to factor this in. The point is to draw attention to something other than the alluring brightness of the activity, the flavoursome intensity of the experience; to draw attention to the live connection made between activities in participants' minds, that elusive, magical moment when a new thought appears.

Quite simply, Odyssey journeys are about increasing participants' sensitivity to this, so they can notice a new idea appearing – perhaps to their mind, perhaps to another's. Simple enough to state, but tricky to discern in the usual hustle and bustle of a workshop or classroom.

From my experience, the way to discern whether this is happening qualitatively with a group of people, students, participants—whether children or adults—is three-fold:

- the general quality of listening improves,

- the number of insights or breakthroughs increases,
- remarkable behaviours emerge.

These are the consequences of a journey well taken. The basic structure provides an opportunity for surprise, for novelty – not just for the challenge the individual activities themselves present, but also the challenge to associate their unique juxtaposition. An Odyssey for sure, but these aren't objectives that can be targeted directly.

We may have an activity that attempts to focus on any one of these objectives directly, as in the **Aha!** moment which sensitises participants to the moment when a new idea flashes into the mind, but this is akin to the learning objectives declared at the beginning of a lesson or a training session, eg *By the end of this lesson, students will be able to factorise quadratic equations,* or some such thing. This kind of declaration works for knowledge and skills, but doesn't serve us well with awareness. How many mission statements by schools and companies have you come across that read like naïve target-setting or border on arrogance, which fall short in practice in the real world? We don't wish to succumb to such an error.

We must recognise that the three-fold qualities we discern above (quality of listening, insights, and emergent behaviour) aren't like objectives we can aim for directly. They're more like incredibly valuable side-products, human qualities we may discern as a consequence which emerge from our activities. Again, structurally, we may parallel the activities, and their juxtaposition; the participants, and their unique engagement; and the practical means of interaction, and the quality consequences which emerge as a result.

What are the limitations of writing about Learning Grids?

In terms of reading and writing, the social dimension's rather restricted. The book brings me closer to you, but you remain well out of reach to me as I write. I can't hear you, or respond to your thinking. Nevertheless, there's a 'space between' us.

In a partnered dance, this 'space between' is the energetic movement of bodies, the emotional interplay, perhaps the spiritual communion. In a congregation or a lecture hall, it's the quality and object of attention, the mutual engagement of feeling. It's the state of harmony or disorder between us all on this planet.

You're the active mind at this very moment. And though you're reading what appear to be my words, they're not. They're just squiggles on the page which you interpret with your own semantic web. We share a similar lexicon; our maps of language match more or less, but some words jar; the use of punctuation sometimes swerves the meaning into a different direction; the terminology can sometimes rub against your own predilection, your own taste. That's partly why Leon and I have settled on this structure for this book, as our different styles will probably appeal to different readers.

The Space Between is a term for the mental attitude, the state of being that honours the actual space in which we're immersed, in our bodies, hearts and minds. We tend to get carried away with our ideas and thoughts, even when we are in a group together. The Learning Grid attempts to bring us closer to the actual current reality, embedded as we are physically in the world, and psychologically in society.

When it comes to the social dimension of this book, I know Leon's open to inviting participants to submit ideas for new books in the Treasure Trove series. And, of course, if we're still alive when you read this, we're contactable via the publisher, and available to meet in the real world, to conduct Learning Grid sessions and foster greater connection in terms of individual learning, and social engagement.

I hope your journey through this book provides you with experiences that invoke insights. Although we believe this is brought out more in person, I hope we've gone some way in crossing this divide between reader and writer.

Create your own Odyssey Grid

Before we give a step-by-step outline of what it takes to create your own Learning Grid, here are some heuristics:

- Be genuine. The activities presented haven't been presented because they're some kind of mechanical fulfilment of a course objective—in other words; some disembodied, objective exercises—they're experiences which you're providing to enlighten and delight participants. Make yours personal.
- Be vulnerable. Include activities because they interest you deeply. When you engage participants, find a response which appeals to you directly, even if this departs from your original design brief.
- Be aware. What may be evoked by the activities, as a result, is an internal awareness, a social cohesion. The location of the learning is in you, or (if the journey is undertaken as a group) in—and between—the participants. It's the participants' learning journey which is important, of which you're one.
- Be open. Make the learning fresh – in participants' minds, and in yours.

With these guidelines in mind, especially those which relate to how you intend the actual social experience to turn out (see **Intention Not Expectation**), follow the steps below to create your Odyssey Grid.

Leon's version

1 Decide how many categories you want – this defines the number of columns and shapes.
2 Decide how many rows you want – this defines the number

of colours and iterations of shapes. Steps 1 and 2 define the size of the grid.

3 Create pieces yourself using coloured card, or print out pieces using the downloadable templates available on line.[16] Organise the pieces into different piles of the same shape. Make sure the Heading Row shapes are the same colour (I like using black), and that the Destination Row shapes are blank.

4 Put aside the group of blank shapes for your Destination Row.

5 Choose category headings, write these on your Heading Row shapes if necessary, and put these aside.

6 For each category, devise content for each piece in the same shape as the category heading, and choose an intriguing related heading or graphic to put on each piece. If you're short of time or inspiration, you can draw on an expanding range of available Odyssey Grid content in the Treasure Trove series, of which this book's a part.[17]

7 Lay out your Heading Row pieces on the floor or on a table, and arrange grid pieces randomly below them in an Odyssey Grid formation.

8 Place your Destination Row pieces at the bottom.

9 I recommend taking a photograph of your grid or making a sketch of it at this stage, so that when you come to put it up on the wall of a room, it's easy to remember where each piece goes. Alternatively, stick the pieces on to a portable display board that you can put up and take down easily.

The reason I don't take into account some of the parameters that David does in approaching his design (eg timing of activities) is that I don't necessarily envisage the whole board being covered in a session or series of sessions. Just because the board's there doesn't mean it's got to be explored in its entirety. Sometimes less is more. I therefore see timing as flexible – with quality of encounter with the content being paramount. I find things work out better if I take this approach. More's covered in more depth — often with earlier steps taking longer, and later ones suddenly becoming easier — as the learning curve takes on a more vertical slope.

It's something you'll have to gauge from experience; and engage with in a way that suits your purpose, situation, personality – while also considering how an Odyssey Grid works best.

David's version

1 Ascertain the conditions of the journey: the time allotted to conduct the journey, the purpose of the journey, and the number of participants.

2 Estimate the size of Learning Grid based on activities anywhere between five and thirty minutes each. This doesn't need to be a square grid. A rectangle will work just as well. The size of the grid depends on the amount of time the participants have, and how long each activity takes. A 4x4 grid, with activities ranging from a few minutes to half an hour each, might take around three hours. If you only have two, you can still use the grid – just limit that session's participants to four or five choices at most, perhaps starting off with four, and adding in a bonus choice halfway through to spice things up.

3 Choose the activities. This can be tricky, so try working from the bottom up. Consider the activities you want to end with at the bottom of the Learning Grid. Layer supporting activities above this, so participants have a chance of appreciating the lower activities. Make sure the starting top row contains activities that are easy enough for participants to jump into, that also set the tone for the whole learning experience. Remember to include an **Introduction** or **Explanation** activity as the top left grid piece! In setting out your grid, you may find it useful to

include different types of activities. Categorise your activities accordingly as you see fit. Don't get religious about this. Categorisation is secondary; the activity is primary.

4 Once you're happy with the mix of content and activity types, assign each grid piece a colour and shape. Draw on the guide given on pages 58–59 or devise your own. Downloadable templates are available on line,[18] or you can create your own. It's important to note that this skill in categorisation, and subsequent decoding, isn't a primary learning objective in the Learning Grid. Categorisation's overplayed in education. For example, philosophy's heavily biased towards those gifted with linguistic intelligences. All too often, wordplay obfuscates the opportunity for young students to get involved at the conceptual level – something they return to with vigour later in life. The Learning Grid can open up conceptual exploration to a wider range of learner styles.

5 Cut out shapes from assorted coloured card; and arrange them vertically, so each strand contains a variety of activities. For example, avoid all the games aligning in one column, and all the videos in another. Ensure there's variety in each vertical thread. I tend to arrange a meta-thread which sequences commentaries or activities about the Learning Grid itself. I then have (very) loose themes arranged vertically, with more mainstream and traditionally accepted threads, and more personal and unverified explorations. Again, don't be religious about this. It's more of a hint, a flavour, an impressionistic categorising – something participants can talk about afterwards over drinks, not a syllogistic problem which has a single concrete solution.

6 Stick the activities directly on a wall or display board, or attach them to strings hung securely from the ceiling so they lie against the wall. Take a photo.

7   You're ready to go! Remember – whatever the individual
    activities may be, it's their juxtaposition which may give
    rise to a new thought. As the guide, you're preparing
    participants for the deeper concepts or skills at the bottom
    of the grid which you wish to share, but the learning that
    arises on the way may prove more valuable to everyone.

Enjoy learning how to make your own grid. It's more of a craft
than a science or an art; design rather than engineering or artistry.
You can only tell if it works when it's tested, so don't get too
heavy on yourself in your first designs. And besides, the responsibility of the learning is centred more on the group. It's their job
to make it interesting. You can provide what you think are the
most interesting activities—and juxtapose them to give the most
fertile associations—but with a deadbeat group or on a dead-end
day, this may turn out rather flat. The design is a marriage of
preparation and implementation. It's an iterative process. Your
designs will improve with practice.

Design your own version

Have these approaches sparked off some new ideas? We very
much hope so! The Odyssey Grid is very flexible, and if you feel
inspired to develop something that will work for you, in your
particular context, go right ahead.

Facilitate an Odyssey journey

How does it work?

Learning Grids are primarily designed as a group learning experience. Journeyers may be students in an educational situation, managers on a training course, or participants in a workshop. The group is facilitated by a guide who introduces the grid – and subsequently, the activities the group has chosen.

To begin, the guide usually picks the first item which is normally termed **Introduction**, though it may be named **Explanation** or **Opportunity**, which we recommend placing at the top left of the grid as a general rule. Participants can choose subsequent stopping points.

As a guide, you can reveal as much or as little about the grid as you wish. For example, you could introduce David's grid as follows:

This is the Learning Grid. Each item is an activity, a game, a puzzle, a definition, a video – who's to know? The colour and shape connect up different activities by type or category, and perhaps you'll start seeing what the pattern is, and this may guide your choice of activity.

The grid's designer has put their most interesting or insightful or useful ideas at the bottom. But—as with all things of great value—they can be tricky to understand or appreciate. Thus, there are a bunch of other activities above to provide the conceptual materials required, so that by the time you get to the bottom, you might comprehend the bottom activities better.

The rule is, you can only choose an activity in the rows below the one you have already chosen.

So, start at the top and work your way down – but don't just drill straight down, you may want to get a broader view by picking activities in other columns. Hopefully, if you've chosen well, paid attention, and completed the activities; by the time we get to the bottom, we'll have a good chance of understanding what lies down there.

Since you're picking each item, the path we choose will be unique to us, here and now. I'll be asking if you notice any patterns between the activities. This means the journey's live to me too, since although I know each activity, the combination will be unique, and new associations will appear in our minds. I mean that honestly – this could give us a new insight not even the designer was aware of. This is our unique Odyssey.

You're encouraged to create a map of your experiences, a personal account of the sequence of activities. You can copy the title, draw pictures, use coloured markers, draw arrows, make notes – anything to record your experience. In this way, you'll have a personal record of your Odyssey through the Learning Grid.

Any questions? No? In which case, it's your turn to choose the next activity – from the first row, of course.

Perhaps a member of the group asks what **Odyssey** means, and in this case, if it happens to be an activity in the grid, highlighted as an example, it could become the first item the group chooses. You'd then either recollect the material for the **Odyssey** activity and explain it to the group or present your own take on it – and so the Odyssey journey begins!

After each activity, give participants time to record their experience, and any associations that are generated between activities. This has the effect of enabling self-reflection, as well as giving a moment for you to collect your thoughts.

Who's in control?

As facilitator, you must let go of control. Your job is merely to share. Should the participants engage well, they'll take themselves—and you—on a journey to where you've already been, or, inspirationally, to a completely new space.

As facilitator, demonstrate to the participants the quality of listening—internal and external—that's expected of them. Limit your words to explaining exercises, and facilitating inner exploration. Experience the exploration with them. Encourage cooperative guidance. This may appear counter-intuitive, because in most courses the person facilitating the training or lesson knows the material, and it's their job to express and explain it. Consider your standard training day or school or university course – and the chances are you think of a talking head.

To elicit the best Odyssey journey experience, you must have the self-discipline to reverse the expectation – and not talk! Your job's to set out the experiences, then listen to the responses evoked, no matter how much the participants want explanations – demand them even!

Both of us have certainly failed in this regard – we've both found ourselves filling the empty space between activities with our own thoughts. It's very difficult to resist a classful of Chinese students – students who wait dutifully for their teacher to present associations and connections, logic and reason. David's even had to go so far as to write up, 'I am not your teacher', on the board, which confronted them with something of a cultural shock. We've both found Maieutic Questioning (page 71) and Wait Times (page 73) useful as tools to help curb the desire to intervene.

What's the proper use of questions?

What's significant to both versions of the Odyssey journey is the process of mutual exploration. Not only can participants deepen their understanding of themselves and one another through this process, but as facilitator you have an opportunity to help create a journey that's meaningful, original, and evolutionary – for the participants *and* for yourself.

Thus, don't use questions to elicit specific knowledge. Use them to encourage genuine exploration. It's not so much about whether you use open or closed questions, but about pointing in directions that you're not sure about – to the open spaces.

One of the hardest tasks for a guide is to not answer participants' questions directly. In some cases this is necessary – mainly to define the rules of an activity. In the realm of connecting activities, a guide must let the participants fend for themselves. It may look like the participants are thrashing about as if drowning, but this is often a result of taking away their customary dependence on authority. To find their own voice, they need to trust one another. Let their questions and answers come from their peers. Observe.

Further techniques to improve interaction are given in the Variations on Questioning Section on page 71 because they're common to both Learning Grid structures featured in this book – and check out **How Do Questions Work?** in the Activities Section.

Who gets to choose what activity is next?

A group of participants may have questions on how exactly the next activity is chosen. This question may be answered by the guide, by the group itself, or by an item in the grid itself (eg **Who Chooses?** in the Collaboration Grid). This is part of the learning experience, the ability of individuals within a group to navigate the social sea in which they're immersed.

What do the colours and shapes signify?

Leon uses colours as navigational aids, rather than as pointers to activity types. For this book, David chose colours and shapes to tease out subtle connections between activities. The colour version is available on line at www.odysseygrids.com. Sometimes the connections were obvious, sometimes the decision was instinctive. For other grids he's designed, he's chosen colours and shapes to indicate more obvious qualities, for instance:

- Red – physical activity, raw and direct;
- Orange – emotional, feeling, sensing;
- Yellow – knowledge-based, perception;
- Green – force of will, decision-making;
- Blue – words, communication;
- Violet – awareness, consciousness.

- Circle – observation, drawing attention, usually a subtle point;
- Triangle – incremental activity, potential to become skilful, a game;
- Square – video, computer activity;
- Diamond – lecture, presentation, definition;
- Star – startling, shocking, a puzzle.

These aren't exclusive of course – he's used zigzags and spirals to indicate different qualities to which he's wanted to draw attention. It's a question of what works in terms of facilitating connections between the activities. That's the point.

How can we keep track of where we are on the grid?

Activities that have been conducted can be marked with a sticker, paper clip or sticky note. This isn't necessary for smaller grids because participants generally remember the different experiences they've gone through; but with larger grids, and with long breaks between sessions, marking the grid is essential.

If participants have been encouraged to make a map of their own journeys, this can also provide a way to keep track of the paths they've taken, translating the Learning Grid into a more personal account. Some participants' maps may be useful for the group, with the order of sequences marked in case this is required, tabulated with date and outcomes – another benefit of having a diverse range of learning styles and personalities in a group.

If using the Session Section Grid (page 82), particularly when lessons are delivered to more than one group and span several sessions, it's vital to keep a note of what activities each group has done and reveal the activities that each group has experienced before that group's session.

How do you facilitate connections between the activities?

The quality of association depends very much on the tone you set as a guide. Whatever level participants are at and however forgiving or demanding you are as a guide, the basic philosophy behind the Learning Grid is **Not Knowing**. It's very easy for a teacher of knowledge to be demanding because they know exactly the material they are talking about – engineering, mathematics, history. However, it's much harder to hone a demanding attitude when we don't know the philosophy of maths, or the theory of management; to balance rigour with openness – but this is what distinguishes a good guide.

If using David's version, where categories are implicit rather than explicit, some participants may start noticing a pattern—that the red grid pieces have something in common, that there's a connection between the diamond-shaped grid pieces, for instance—so they slowly piece together a code. Celebrate this as a learning point that can be shared with the whole group and riff on it, eg *What do the other shapes or colours signify for each of us?*

How do you know when a Learning Grid is going well?

Enjoyment is one way of telling, but this can take many forms. We tend to emphasise the noisy form of enjoyment, which we normally associate with children or boisterous teenagers. However, there are other ways in which we enjoy learning.

Because our Learning Grids are firmly immersed in **Social-Learning**, the following three social qualities are good indicators that the learning environment is thriving:

- the general quality of listening improves,
- the number of insights or breakthroughs increases,
- remarkable behaviours emerge.

The first can be discerned in terms of silence. How quiet are the participants? Are they quiet, but some distracted, following their own thinking? What is the intensity of their attention? Think of a theatre performance, when the audience is in the palm of the actor's hand, following every word, every inflection – rapt attention. The more people attending to the same thing, the more intense the attention, the quieter the group.

The second is a simple rate of measure. Participants are encouraged to reflect on their learning, to draw out insights they may have about activities. If the learning environment's thriving, the rate of **Aha!**s increases.

The third's the most subtle to discern, unless it happens to you directly. The learning doesn't remain as a thought, but manifests as action – an action which is uncharacteristic of you. Being able to perform a mathematical calculation you'd previously thought impossible, for example, or becoming a spokesperson for the class without asking for it or it formally being suggested – when things happen—almost magically, **Inspirationally**—they happen first, and then you think about them.

These three social qualities—quality of listening, rate of insight, emergent behaviour—characterise a thriving social learning environment.

Getting the right balance

Choosing the activities for the grid is an artistic skill, and in his early days developing the Odyssey Grid idea, David made fabulous errors. This is, of course, part of the journey – the ability to learn from mistakes. The trick is choosing just the right balance of challenge (see **Csiklets**).

The right balance. An oft-quoted phrase, and much abused from our perspective. It may sound like wisdom to be able to decide where the balance is, but on which side do we err?

For the most part, we deem the correct wisdom to be the one where people find balance in life, and thus meet with success. They change the things that can be changed, and by doing so, they develop personally while society improves in some way. As David says,

> *Although I was a model student while at school and university, I mentally questioned what was going on. In my late twenties, I eventually recognised that I always took a step too far—psychologically at least—with people. I wasn't content with meeting the boundary of what was correct. I always had to question it. And one way to question a boundary, as any parent knows, is to step over the boundary, and see what happens.*
>
> *This ability to take one step too far has proven to be a very useful learning method—informing how I play GO, learn t'ai chi and dance Argentine tango—which has brought an aliveness to my classes as a mathematics teacher. I often play in the area of not knowing, playing to my weaknesses not my strengths.*

The Learning Grid, by its very nature, can have this quality. The guide's a learning coach, not an expert teacher; the participants aren't passive receivers, but active explorers. Where are the boundaries between the participants? And how are they found?

Because the centre of learning has shifted to the embodied group of participants – these specific people in this specific room, the boundaries shift – they're defined by the experience. We become the conditions for one another. And who's to say what can and can't be changed?

We must be courageous enough to learn how to engage with

one another. A polite mentality can mean participants remain in themselves – reserved, not wishing to impose upon one another. A more aggressive approach can mean participants are pushy and compete with one another. Check out the American and British versions of *The Apprentice* to see this played out. Between these two, I'd like to encourage forceful listening, courageous inquisitiveness, a militant generosity of spirit.

In most of the Learning Grids David designs, there's come to be a vertical column that places the learning group in the wider context of society. This not only contextualises the overall topic of the Learning Grid, it enables participants to question the design of the content – to question the conditions of what's presented to them. Participants are invited to bring into play aspects of the world which haven't been invited in directly, but which they feel might be significant to other participants.

Learning Grids ought to be placed against the ongoing, wider challenges in the world. This could be to place before the teenager the current edge of scientific exploration regarding artificial intelligence, or current thinking about the philosophy of mathematics – what is mathematics after all? It could be to bring participants face to face with the necessary fact that we need to improve our ability to listen to one another.

Much of the preparation's about choosing just the right balance of challenge. And this goes for the participants too – deciding how much mental challenge one can take. In fact, this is perhaps one of the deepest lessons we put ourselves through in the journey of our lives. Do we accept the status quo of argumentative politics and environmental degradation?

God, grant me the serenity to accept the things I cannot change, the courage to change the things I can, and the wisdom to know the difference.
Reinhold Niebuhr

Using Kagan Structures with groups[19]

What are Kagan Structures?

Kagan Structures are strategies codified primarily by American educationalist Dr Spencer Kagan to help facilitate cooperative learning among groups. The strategies are ways of organising activities – usually in pairs or groups of 3–6 students. What's unique about them is the fact that they're content-free and repeatable. That means they can be applied in many situations or contexts, across all subjects and educational programmes to develop teamwork, thinking and social skills, as well as the primary purpose of engaging with specific topics.

Why use Kagan Structures?

They directly and effectively address the interpersonal and academic educational needs of individuals in groups.

How do they do this? Kagan says it's all about PIES:[20]

- Positive interdependence;
- Individual accountability;
- Equal participation;
- Simultaneous interaction.

Together, they support collaborative learning, and are ideally suited to facilitate the social aspect of group learning which is such an important part of an Odyssey journey when used with classes and groups of participants.

Each structure contains a blueprint for a short group activity. Longer cooperative learning interventions can take place across a term or 10-week period, eg Co-Op Co-Op.

How do they work?

Here are two examples.

Jot Thoughts (Kagan, 2009)

Teammates "cover the table," writing ideas on slips of paper.

Setup: Students each have multiple slips of paper (eg pre-cut sticky notes, cut-up bond paper).

1 Teacher names a topic, sets a time limit, and provides think time (eg, In three minutes, how many questions can you write that have the answer 17? What are ways we could reduce poverty?).
2 Students write and announce as many ideas as they can in the allotted time, one idea per slip of paper.
3 Each slip of paper is placed in the center of the table; students attempt to "cover the table" (no slips are to overlap).

Numbered Heads Together (Kagan, 2009)

Teammates put their "heads together" to reach consensus on the team's answer. Everyone keeps on their toes because their number may be called to share the team's answer.

Setup: Teacher prepares questions or problems to ask teams.

1 Students number off.
2 Teacher poses a problem and gives think time. (Example: "How are rainbows formed? Think about your best answer.")
3 Students privately write their answers.
4 Students stand up and "put their heads together," showing answers, discussing, and teaching each other.
5 Students sit down when everyone knows the answer or has something to share.
6 Teacher calls a number. Students with that number answer

simultaneously using:
- AnswerBoard Share,
- Choral Practice,
- Finger Responses,
- Chalkboard Responses,
- Response Cards,
- Manipulatives.

7 Classmates applaud students who responded.

Variations

Paired Heads Together

Students are in shoulder partner pairs. After teacher asks a question, pairs huddle to improve the answers they have each written. Teacher then calls for either As or Bs to share their best answer with their face partner.

Traveling Heads Together

Traveling Heads starts the same as Numbered Heads, but when the teacher calls a number, the students with that number on each team stand, then "travel" to a new team to share their answers. For fun, seated students beckon for a standing student to join their team.

Stir-the-Class

Teams stand around the outside of the class with spaces between teams. Teammates stand shoulder-to-shoulder. The teacher poses a question, then students write their own answers on an AnswerBoard or slip of paper. Teammates huddle to reach consensus, then unhuddle when done. The teacher selects a number and tells students with that number how many teams to rotate forward to share their answer.

There are over 200 structures in the Kagan collections, but you can come up with your own variations yourself once you're familiar with them and how they work. For instance:

Think-Write-RallyRobin

Students are given individual think time, after which—and only after which, not before—they write down their thoughts and ideas before forming pairs and taking turns to respond orally to share what they've each come up with.

Think-Pen-Pair-Share

Students are given individual think time, after which—and only after which, not before—they're given the chance to scribe, write, doodle, map or draw ideas (hence 'Pen' rather than 'Write' or 'Draw' or any other term which might be limiting). They then take turns to respond orally to discuss what they've each come up with. Finally, they share the result of their discussion within a larger team.

How do Kagan Structures fit into an Odyssey journey?

Because of their open-ended quality, Kagan Structures are ideally suited for use on Odyssey journeys. In fact, an Odyssey journey can be designed around teaching a group a bunch of them for the first time. You might even want to colour-code grid pieces to reflect types of Structures, eg Structures that promote classbuilding (eg Find Someone Who or StandUp–HandUp–PairUp), social skills (most if not all of them), or thinking skills (eg Jot Thoughts or Think-Write-RoundRobin). Kagan Structures have been suggested individually for Leon's grids in the Activities Section, and collectively for David's below – you'll want to choose the most appropriate one for your students and their learning needs, eg social skills, thinking skills or knowledge building.[21] Whatever you decide, preparation is definitely worthwhile here.

Suggested Kagan Structures for use with David's grids

David's Learning and Collaboration Grids

Many of the activities in these grids are designed for individual reflection and practice. Think-Pair-Share is recommended as a potential structure to use for further discussion. You might want to use more energised structures such as Pairs Compare or Mix-Freeze-Group to encourage participants to explore further. The results of their reflection can be shared in pairs or groups. Structures such as RallyTable, Three-Step Interview and RoundTable are ideally suited. Others such as Opinion Sages or GiveOne–GetOne would work well for activities which result in differences of opinion, or have multiple possible answers. Share insights on the journeys undertaken as a whole and the individual connections made between activities via structures such as Carousel Feedback, Team Up! or Team-2-Team, among other possibilities.[21a]

Algebra Grid

The activities in this grid fall roughly into two camps: theory and practice. For the former, similar structures to those listed above are likely to work well. For the latter, Rally Coach, Team-Pair-Solo, RoundTable Consensus or Showdown are our suggestions. Of course, you're free to choose your own.[21b]

Things to be aware of

As Dr Theodore Panitz, a specialist in interactive/collaborative approaches to teaching and learning has pointed out,

> *Collaboration is a philosophy of interaction and personal lifestyle whereas cooperation is a structure of interaction designed to facilitate the accomplishment of an end product or goal.*[22]

Panitz believes that in the US tradition, influenced by John Dewey, there is a tendency to privilege product-based evaluation and cooperative learning, whereas in the UK, there is a tendency to privilege process and collaboration. In this book, David's approach tends towards collaborative learning; Leon's towards cooperative learning. At the end of the day, we aim to meet in the middle. The trick is to set up structures and activities so they combine the best of both worlds.

As Panitz notes,

> There are so many benefits which accrue from both ideas that it would be a shame to lose any advantage gained from the student-student-teacher interactions created by both methods. We must be careful to avoid a one-size-fits-all mentality when it comes to education paradigms.
>
> ... I think it behooves teachers to educate themselves about the myriad of techniques and philosophies which create interactive environments where students take more responsibility for their own learning and that of their peers. Then it will become possible to pick and choose those methods which best fit a particular educational goal or community of learners.

To make your life easier, there are a number of resources available from the Kagan Online website such as timers, random selectors and Learning Chips for use with structures, or you can make your own.

When collaborative learning works, it's like a jazz performance, in which performers are all jamming creatively, to a shared agreed structure. The structure allows all four vital interlinked components of PIES to be expressed. Planning for a collaborative experience is essential – but when in the moment, it's important to remember to let go. Preparation is vital, but as the great saxophonist, Charlie Parker, is reputed to have said,

> ... when you finally get up there on the bandstand, forget all that and just wail!

Variations

Variations on timing

Standard timings

It's useful to set a time limit for when you intend to reach a solution. In a classroom or meeting session, the time limits for completing each segment of the journey tend to be part of the schedule – defined either by the end of a session or the interval between one session and the next. Within a given time frame, you can explore one or more grid pieces, but remember to allocate enough time to explore the connections between activities. If you want to vary things, here are some ideas…

Fast Food Interaction

What happens if you give yourself only 30 seconds to come up with as many ideas as possible?

Procrastinator Pleaser

What if you condense all the thinking you've done about the problem from the time you first engaged with it to 30 seconds starting… now!?

Meditative Approach

Cultivate mental discipline by setting aside five minutes at the beginning and end of your day to work on an Odyssey problem.

Ariadne's Thread

Try completing a line of thought in a precisely-timed session, or extending a line of thought continuously across a series of such sessions, starting exactly where you left off last time. The benefit is to work on precise recall of each stopping point, and the line of argument that you took to reach it, and hit the ground running to continue your journey along your chosen avenue of enquiry relentlessly, like a marathon runner, until you get to the final destination of your Odyssey journey.

A One-Hour Journey

This works well with any size Odyssey Grid, but the number of moves should be limited, to allow participants to navigate the grid in an hour. The more moves there are, the less time there will be to explore each one in depth. It's particularly useful in a business setting to unleash creativity or come up with solutions in a problem-solving session. Journeys can be undertaken by individuals, pairs or groups, with a Kagan Structure like Travelling Heads Together used at the end for sharing the outcomes of group journeys or Inside Outside Circle, perhaps, used to share individual journeys.

Variations on questioning

Maieutic Questioning

As noted on page 28, maieutic questioning or dialogue is a process in which the questioner acts as a midwife to a learner, in order to awaken latent knowledge, or create links between existing knowledge, values, and new information – with the questioner acting as facilitator, or extractor; rather than an imposer of knowledge, just as Plato reports Socrates doing. But does this mean everyone should reinvent the wheel through this process?

Sicilian sociologist Danilo Dolci has been nominated twice for the Nobel Peace Prize as a result of his work using maieutic dialogue to break the hold of the Mafia in Sicily. In his outline for a new educational centre, he noted that

> ... it's impossible for everyone to rediscover everything... one must look beyond the Socratic fable—and beyond the Socratic model

itself—and pick out the essential point: how is one to deepen or extend the power of observation, to exercise it and give it expression in various ways, to deepen and develop personal experience in order to try to solve the problems which face us in everyday life.

One can go far by working together to find a valid basis for research, work and verification: one interest may lead to another in a never-ending chain.

A work of education, like a work of art, comes into being as it develops and it evolves in a way which is by definition unforeseeable.[23]

When used in the spirit of this statement, Odyssey journeys involving maieutic questioning have the potential to develop wisdom through a process of co-discovery.

Unending Line of Questioning

Let your interaction with the grid be limited to *only* asking questions. Allow time to flow freely while you pursue a series of questions, each question leading to another question, and another… potentially ad infinitum.

Clean Language Questioning

Clean Language Questioning is a question-led interaction process devised by David Grove in 1989.[24] It is used both in therapy, education and corporate training.[25] It's a highly effective technique for achieving clarity and transformation in behaviour in line with clear goals the answerers had previously defined. It's a technique that can be used particularly effectively to elicit internalised knowledge that might otherwise not have been brought to the fore. Facilitating the move of internalised knowledge from the subconscious part of journeyers' minds to a more conscious level of thinking – and having them verbalise it has multiple benefits: it fixes learning, maximises brain power, and aids retention. Simple questions like 'What kind of x is that x?' or 'Is there anything else about that x?', where 'x' stands for something a journeyer has said, can elicit real insights. Clean language can also be used to help journeyers reflect on their own individual way or ways of thinking, of learning and of making connections. Questions like 'Whereabouts is x?' when related to thought processes, or feelings related to learning well or unproductive behaviour can help unpack successful individual learning strategies, as well as decode the things that get in the way of the successful navigation of pathways to enlightenment.[26] And why not transform the experience by teaching journeyers some basic clean language questions, and get them to practise using them on you when they want to draw out more clues from a cultural riddle, puzzle or challenge?

Wait Times[27]

It's useful if everyone—participants as well as facilitators—develops the ability to pause at will for around three seconds before answering a question. It can also be useful to pause this long before asking a question. It's not a question of creating a rule to follow religiously – making it a habit would probably disempower the strategy from its meaningful use. It's about using pauses consciously to allow **The Space Between** to develop.

Empowering participants to use pauses to highlight thought phrases—and/or for emphasis—can bring an added level of insight into the activity that's well worth spending time cultivating.

Variations on journeying

Standard interaction

In a standard interaction, a facilitator sets out the procedures and, starting from the top left shape below the Header Row, participants take turns in choosing the points which will define the path of a unique Odyssey journey. Either during the journey, or at the end, participants think about the connections between categories; the end goal being to come up with a previously unknown conclusion after the final arrival at a shape in the bottom row.

The Secret Revelation Journey

Instead of displaying random words visibly, write them on the inside of flaps, or on the back of shapes, with the word only revealed when the participant choosing lifts the flap, or turns the shape over.

Individual Journeys

Using the Secret Revelation setup described above, allow individual members of a group to take individual Random Odyssey Journeys by facilitating individual interactions, rather than group ones.

Seek the Light[28]

Using the Secret Revelation setup described above, get journeyers to select a shape, and before turning it over, visualise the shape placed on a door at the top of a staircase which they have to climb to get to. Beyond the door is a very bright light. There's a sense of mounting excitement—bliss, even—as they gradually climb the stairs. As they turn the shape over, and the word's revealed, the door vanishes, and they're catapulted into the light, which envelops and permeates them. Encourage journeyers to visualise what images appear spontaneously from that experience, and get them to verbalise descriptions of them as fast as they can.

Explore what the quality of the results are when drawing pictures or using movement to capture the mental images.

Paired Interactions

See **Textango**, for example.

Symmetrical Journeys

Shapes are chosen symmetrically in pairs or groups of four, for instance:

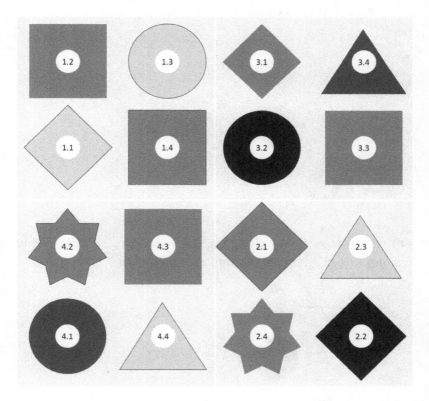

The moves between groups happen via a jump to a new grid piece which is similar to the last in either shape or colour. Connections can be made between groups and between grid pieces in each group. This variation works best on Odyssey Grids that have been set up truly randomly. The order in which activities within each group are done can be varied. Planning ahead is vital if you want a consistent journey. If you're prepared for a bit of turbulence, add in a stop on a single piece where necessary – it might reveal a particularly interesting insight.

Simple Cumulative Step Journeys

On the first go, standard rules apply; but from the second go, the horizontal and vertical moves are to the shape two away from the base shape that has been arrived at in the previous go, as shown here:

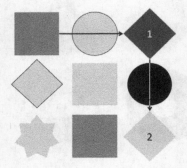

or two jumps away, travelling via shapes which are similar either in colour or shape in alternation, as shown here:

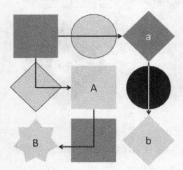

Random Cumulative Step Journeys

Any Journey Variation, chosen at will by participants.

From Inside the Box to Outside the Box

In one style of workshop, the **Explanation** activity appears as a box on a chair before the audience. We begin in an unorthodox way – passing ourselves off as attendees, turning up and registering like everyone else. You should try it, it's a lot of fun. A big sign declares the workshop begins at 9am, and most times the attendees seat themselves dutifully. So far, we've not had to spark interest in the box at the front of the room ourselves. Members of the group motivate themselves and others to investigate the box, whether it's through curiosity (the workshop title 'Exploring Curiosity' is a rather large hint), or through the chagrin of having to wait, and complaining about the organisers (which, as one of the organisers seated in the audience, takes a little self-discipline to listen to). In the end, it is the box which contains the explanation, and it refers to the starting piece **Opportunity** on the grid on the wall, and so the journey has begun.

Variations on structures

Variations in stance

Put a board together with a clear educational end in mind, the point of which is to teach set material in an intriguing way, and generate strong connections between existing and newly acquired knowledge. This teaches content primarily, and thinking vicariously.

Put a board together experimentally, with seemingly unconnected elements. This teaches thinking primarily, and content vicariously. It links to the I Ching, inviting serendipity and randomness into the proceedings.

To explore this approach further, take a Random Odyssey Journey.

The Random Odyssey Journey

Imagine one day you walk down a bustling street in the 'downtown' area of a busy metropolis. You see a cab and hail it. You get in, but apart from knowing that you're in a cab, on a journey, knowing you need to get somewhere by a certain time, you don't know where your final destination will be. You'll get there via a route that is worked out collaboratively between you and the driver. Where that route will lead you is unclear, but you'll be guided by random signposts on the way, and see what happens.

This Random Odyssey Journey variation is structured precisely as this kind of journey.

This idea might seem surreal, even frightening, in an educational context, but as an antidote to (and with the potential to be delivered alongside) prescribed curriculum-based learning, it can offer just as structured an approach to the development of lateral and deep-level thinking.

The secret of this variation lies in the fact that the content is not pre-packaged. In fact, in this Random Odyssey Journey variation, all that is loaded on to the basic Odyssey structure is a framework of signposts to destinations as yet unknown.

Benefits

Use this Odyssey structure if you want to:

- develop lateral thinking,
- develop deep thinking,
- develop creative thinking.

Develop lateral thinking by making connections between random words and random categories.

Develop deep thinking by using words regularly as prompts to practise techniques of accessing deep-thinking techniques in a structured, fun way.

Develop creative thinking by making connections, in the moment, between random categories, random words, and the subject of the day.

Want to go on a Random Odyssey Journey?
Here's what we've come up with to get you going:

Setup
Collate the content for your Random Odyssey Grid over the course of a day.

1 Get a notebook and pencil ready.
2 Note the number of columns and rows you're going to use. Decide on the number of pieces you want in your Random Odyssey Grid.
3 Carry these with you throughout the day.
4 Collect words to go in the grid pieces as you go through your day. You may want to limit yourself to three or four words in every section of your day (breakfast, morning routine, break, work, lunch, commute, supper, etc). You may want to start at a certain point, when the first significant word appears and finish when you reach your limit, allowing words to flow into your stream of consciousness as and when they're ready to.

In choosing, go for words that seem significant to you, or stand out. They could be due to the typographical layout of an advertisement in a morning paper, or a headline word in a poster you see in an unusual place, or a word remembered through association during your morning routine, something triggered by a sensory experience during a meal, a word you coin for the particular shape made by the ring the base of a wet tumbler leaves on a surface. The possibilities are endless.
5 When you have collected the number of words you set out

to reach, turn a new page, put down the number of categories you'll need in the Header Row, and put your notebook aside for three months, or long enough to forget the details of where they came from. Make a diary note to revisit your notebook, and note down where you put it, so you can find it easily again.

6 After three months, or whatever your chosen period is, without looking at the previous list of words you've gathered, select category headings to use for each shape type in your Random Odyssey Journey grid Heading Row.

7 Gather these words as before, writing them down in your notebook, and put it aside for another three months, or for long enough to forget the details of how you chose them, and where they came from.

8 After another three months, first retrieve the initial word list, without looking at the categories. Choose as many different shapes as there are columns in your grid; and for each shape, create series of as many different colours as there are rows in your grid, and two extra sets of single shapes for Heading and Destination Rows. Make the Heading Row a different colour to all the other colours you've used in the grid (eg black). Make the Destination Row shapes blank. Put Heading and Destination Row pieces aside. Mix the remaining grid pieces up randomly. Construct your Random Odyssey Journey grid by assigning component words in order to the randomly-arranged coloured shapes. Then apply the words to the shapes in your Heading Row.

9 Assemble the Random Odyssey Journey grid like a Sudoku puzzle, making sure no two pieces of the same colour or shape are directly next to each other.

Taking a Random Odyssey Journey
Use the standard interaction on page 73 or any of the variations

on pages 74–77.

Journeyer's Constant Mystery Heading
Leave one piece blank in the Heading Row for journeyers to fill with their own meaningful content. The rule for this variation is that the choice made remains constant for the whole journey. The choice can be made before the journey starts, or during it.

Facilitator's Constant Mystery Heading
Again, leave one piece blank in the Heading Row, but this time, the facilitator is the one who generates the content. The choice can be made before the journey starts, or during it.

Journeyer's Variable Mystery Heading
As above, but the content for this heading can vary throughout the game. The first choice can be made before the journey starts, or during it.

Facilitator's Variable Mystery Heading
As above, but the content for this heading can vary throughout the game. The first choice can be made before the journey starts, or during it.

Session Section Grid

Students in one of Leon's classes asked to 'have more Odyssey Grid sessions' in the lesson, so this Learning Grid was developed in response:

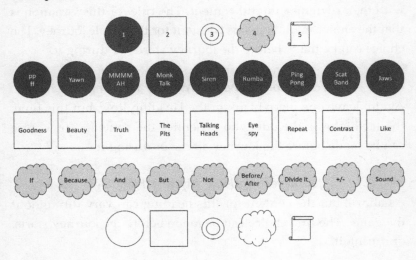

The context here is a course to develop effective voice-centred communication skills. The top row is the Heading Row; the bottom row, the Destination Row. Each lesson contains five activities:

- a vocal warm-up exercise;
- a selection of core verbalising activities related to story-telling;
- work on story structures;
- a selection of verbal structures to incorporate into a story and
- an open-ended connection exercise to evaluate learning in the session.

The central grid has three rows relating to the sections of the class open to students to choose from (1, 2 and 4). We didn't always get to cover all three central sections, but the learning was the richer for it. The inclusion of up to three grid entry points in a session allowed more students to have a turn picking the next activity, which they liked, and which helped them make connections between the learning points at the end of the session, when they were asked to make connections between all five activities they'd experienced in that session. In practice, the shapes were displayed with the labels facing the wall, and were only turned over to reveal what was on them after they'd been chosen, which added to the mystery of the journey.

Variations on content

Categories
Grids can be seen as maps that outline a particular genus, with grid pieces representing different species that are related to it.

Period-specific Odyssey Grids
Grids of any kind can be explored with a particular focus in mind, eg in the context of the Renaissance, the 20th Century, or the Baroque.

Subject-specific Odyssey Grids
Grids can also be explored with a particular subject focus in mind – whether spatial or topical.

An invitation
These are all words. What matters is experience, action. Try hosting an Odyssey session if one isn't available to you to participate in. Invite yourself to one we might be running – we'd be happy to see you, to have you along for the journey, and even to attend a session you're hosting to experience some new ideas for using the system.

In the meantime, we hope you enjoy the Odyssey experience!
David and Leon

Activities

4D (David's version, page 34)

Create a visual illusion where the mind's eye shifts an 'internal' corner to an 'external' one. There's a video on YouTube,[29] which has links to how to make it. You can create your own version from the blank outline and instructions provided below, recreated by kind permission of Peter Dahmen.

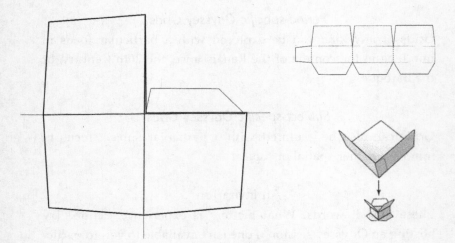

Decorate the inside faces of the half-cube as you wish.
Cut, fold and assemble as illustrated.
Look at the model from above.
Close one eye and move your head.
In which direction does the cube extend?

One pseudo-mathematical explanation is that the illusion is exhibiting an inversion in the fourth dimension; the viewer has reflected an internal corner into an external corner. Compare to how a hand is reflected in a mirror.

The experience relates the shift of perception to shifts in understanding. That is, a shift in conceptual perception can bring about a sudden, remarkable shift in our understanding.

A or B (Collaboration Grid, page 41)

Challenge the participants to find the difference between A **and** B, and A **or** B. They can use the Internet, formal logic, or approach the project artistically. Set a time – say two minutes, and then ask them to share what they have found, without repeating what others have discovered.

For collaboration, we are emphasising the inclusive OR function, rather than the exclusive AND function.

Some discussion on language may follow. In everyday English, we say 'both A and B', meaning all elements of A and all elements of B, which is actually the inclusive OR function; and we say 'either A or B' to mean the exclusive OR function: it is either in A or it is in B, but not both.

It is important to establish what we mean when we connect to other activities. We wish to encourage the mindset that it is possible for two people to be correct even if their perspectives differ. We wish to avoid a mindset which is based on the law of the excluded middle, the exclusive A or B, where only one side is right.

What questions would you ask, in the moment, to extend

the discussion?

Action Cycle (Collaboration Grid, page 41)

Participants are invited to arrange themselves into groups of ten or less, and reach an answer to the following question within the time allotted – normally an hour: "What can be done by next week?"

The process is minimal, but very concentrated. The most important qualities are within the participants, and how they realise their potential—and inherent resources—together, to conceive, commit, and achieve an idealistic objective... idealistic, because often to attempt to achieve it within the framework of a week is deemed impossible given standard behavioural procedures, hence the reliance on one another to pull together – to trust one another, in order to see the objective is achieved.

The rules to conduct an **Action Cycle** are given below, and resources of three colours of card are available on line in the form of graphics to print or pre-made cards.[30]

Green Card

The main question to answer is "What can we (the people in this room now) achieve (just beyond realistic into idealistic) within the week (given our collective resources)?" which can be measured by the following three thresholds, or wows:

- First wow – we achieve consensus on a mutual idealistic objective (even though we may see it differently);
- Second wow – we achieve consensus on commitment (even

though we will all be performing different tasks);

- Third wow, after the group has broken up – we actually do what's needed over the week, and achieve the idealistic objective.

The techniques for achieving the wows involve the five rules of the game, the yellow-red card procedure while in the meeting, and whatever resources and social media are at our disposal during the week.

Yellow Card

The five rules of the game:

1 No oppositional state – yes! (from A or B to both A and B).
2 No brainstorming – observation and insight (just bring what you know, and be sensitive to new ideas that emerge naturally).
3 No splitting – maintain unity (no pairing etc; or postponing positive engagement for afterwards).
4 No pulling – return attention (avoid self-ego-me, past or future; just be present. Just think of the objective, and the steps required to achieve it).
5 No judgement – assume genius or wisdom (evaluate for sure, but just don't think it's foolish).

Red Card

The yellow-red card procedure might be useful to prevent a group from failing itself – everyone agrees to play the game by accepting to uphold the rules of the game, as well as the following two rules:

1 if anyone in the group perceives a rule to be broken, they hold up the yellow card, and the entire group must stop what they are doing, introducing a period of 30 seconds'

silence in which everyone considers their role in what's happening;

2 if anyone in the group flouts the yellow card—or abuses it—any individual may hold up the red card which threatens that the individual leave the group, thus bringing the **action cycle** to an end.

It takes a few minutes to run through the procedure, and the participants can check rules from the cards or copies distributed to each group. The emphasis isn't so much on playing by the rules of the game, but on attempting to put into practice a collaborative mindset, which the activities in the Collaboration Grid have been exercising.

Aha! (David's version, page 34; Collaboration Grid, page 41)

Aha!

Getting an **Aha!** moment is one of the staple objectives of the Learning Grid. It's about facilitating a state in which outside understanding shifts to inside understanding.

Often what's needed is the juxtaposition of things, concepts, activities that seem quite disconnected. Keeping two or more activities in mind without understanding creates the conditions for **Aha!** moments to occur.

What's your experience? What else can help them happen?

In a group setting, participants are invited to consider what constitutes the moment when a new thought pops into their head, when inspiration strikes. After a minute's consideration, they share with their partner for a minute or two, then share with the whole group.

What's important isn't what the definition is, but being sensitive to when it happens mentally. Being open and receptive increases the rate at which **Aha!**s arise if the recipient places themselves in rich learning environments, with people who think differently to themselves.

Algebra (Algebra Grid, page 38)

Challenge students to search for the meaning of algebra for 30 seconds.

Discuss the historical description of the Arabic term, 'al-jabr' – which has been taken to mean 'reunion of broken parts' or 'balancing'.[31]

Discuss the pertinence of this word, and why it was used. The physical mechanics of the balance maps to the centrality of the equal sign, and the adding and removing of weights until the unknown object is on one side, and the measured weights are on the other.

I've distilled three processes to solve equations. They're best clothed in the metaphor provided by other activities (eg **On Yer Bike** or **Arrow And Bow**), but I'll outline them roughly here:

Equal sign: whatever is done to one side of the equation must be done to the other.

x: we're aiming for the unknown to appear by itself on one side of the equal sign, and whatever's on the other side must be our answer.

Simplify: as a general rule, get rid of things furthest away from the x first.

For example:

$$3x + 4 = 25$$

We'd like to aim for x by itself, so let's start by subtracting 4 from the left side, in which case we also need to subtract 4 from the right side too in order to keep both sides equal:

$$3x = 21$$

If we're aiming for x by itself, we need to divide the left side by three, in which case we need to do the same to the right side, leaving us with the answer:

$$x = 7$$

There's no need to explain at this stage – indeed, students at the end of the Learning Grid may be able to express these three processes in their own words, divested of the metaphor through which they've been introduced.

Arrow And Bow (Algebra Grid, page 38)

A metaphor for algebra.

Students must balance the arrow – keep it in the middle. This translates, in solving equations, as maintaining the equal sign. Whatever's done to one side must be done to the other. If seven's added to the left side of the equation, then seven must be added to the other side. A pressure one way must be balanced by a pressure the other way. Balance must be maintained.

Students must aim for the target. In simple problem solving, this means they're aiming for the unknown—usually an x—to be by itself on one side of the equal sign. Whatever's left on the other side is the answer. We're aiming for x on one side and a number on the other side.

Lastly, students must compensate for the conditions when letting off the arrow. The equation changes from its starting point until it hits the target, with x by itself. The target might be distant, in which case there may be multiple steps. The different techniques to learn—brackets etc—are equivalent to learning about airspeed, how dampness affects the tension of the bow, fletching, and so on.

A further way to use the metaphor is to address the nature of the target – whether it's moving or fixed, obvious or camouflaged, for example. Some equations can be rather fearsome.

The important things are: balance, aim, and dealing with the specific conditions.

How can you apply this when working on your next equation?

Attention to Failure (Collaboration Grid, page 41)

A friend of mine noticed this. To go from -6 to +6 requires the addition of +12. This is incremental. In terms of mental states, a person may be feeling down, may experience a hardship; and the way for them to deal with it is to attend to positive things, and gradually come to terms with the hardship or the negative feeling. As we know, we go up, and we go down depending on what occurs.

There's another way. To go from -6 to +6 involves changing the sign. This is done mathematically by multiplying by -1. The psychological aspect of this is to actually be grateful for the negative feeling or the hardship. It's an opportunity to learn. Without it, one wouldn't be aware there was a problem to solve.

Hence, failure's very useful. It's not so much moving on from the failure as soon as possible, but really mining the failure for all it's worth. This results in a conversion, and depends primarily on mental state.

An exercise for this is to think of some of the things that have happened to you that you see as bad; order them in a list of increasing 'disaster'; and then think of the positive versions for the small problems first, and so on, until the larger ones are being converted. For example, you may have broken your leg, which meant you couldn't go in to work; positively, it could have given you a rest, and you could have caught up with some reading. Again, it's not the content per se, but the mental state, which converts negative into positive.

B&W or Black and White (Leon's version, page 17 – Category: Puzzles)

Things are bad for the miller and his daughter. The rains have destroyed the wheat crops, and no one's brought in their wheat to be ground into flour. They've no money to pay the rent, and they don't know what to do. The landlord's ugly, but he's kind – or so he makes out. He makes them an offer. "Chance is a hard thing, so give chance a chance to put things right, eh?" he chuckles. "Have you got a small bag?" The miller nods and brings one out for him. "Look – see where the path out here is full of black and white stones? I'll pick up a couple – one black and one white, and put them in the bag." He bends down, picks up two stones, and puts them in the bag. "If your daughter picks out the white one, I'll let you stay in the mill rent free until the next harvest's in. If she picks out the black one, in lieu of rent, you'll give her hand to me in marriage, and you'll have to earn a living elsewhere." The miller wasn't going to agree at first, but his daughter managed to talk him into it. She'd seen the landlord put two black pebbles in the bag and had hatched a plan. How do you think she managed to get out of the marriage without embarrassing the landlord by revealing he'd cheated, and have her and her father get the good end of the deal?

Recommended Kagan Structures:

(1) **To capture thoughts, ideas or questions participants may have:** Jot Thoughts. (2) **To generate further ideas and discussion:** Think-Pair-Share, Think-Pen-Pair-Share (an original variation) or StandUp–HandUp–PairUp (with RallyRobin or Timed Pair Share). (3) **To promote group discussion and solution:** Numbered Heads Together or Travelling Heads Together. The results could be shared via Team Stand-N-Share, Team Statements or Blackboard Share. For further ideas, see Structure Sequences.[32]

Bracketing (Algebra Grid, page 38)

Bracketing

Demonstrate multiplying out brackets, and perhaps factorising terms.

$3(x + 5) = 21$

$7(x - 3) = 28$

$9(x + 4) = 81$

There are plenty of free resources available on the net,[33] with a solid block of repetitive questions being ideal.

Timing's essential. Twenty-minute blocks enable students to see how well they've done, and to compare their output to others.

Queries should be responded to in terms of the guiding metaphors, if they've been explained: to keep track of the target, to get back on their bike. Otherwise, the teacher must rely on their own more abstract description. The student must attempt, even if it's to fail. The guide shouldn't fall into the trap of feeding the student's anxiety. Their job's to try, and fail if necessary – and in this is a learning experience. Once several attempts have been made, then of course the correct method can be reintroduced – by the guide, or by a fellow student.

Buddhism (David's version, page 34)

Buddhism

The principal tenet of Buddhism—and many Eastern philosophies—is that we're all living in illusion. Translated into something we can use in business, our minds have a capacity to project, to invent, to create the world around us. We then share these illusions for practical purposes. For example, I normally sit on a 'chair', and I'm sure you do too. However, at a certain age we use the object as a hiding space, a house, and all number of creative purposes. Another example: when we visit 'London', there's nothing in the buildings, or the people, that defines what London is, and yet it's useful to use the term and its associations, such as to speak English (except on Oxford Street!), drive on the left, and so on. A third example: a father expects his son to follow his lead, to like his choice of music, support his team; and when the boy comes of age, and chooses his own team, his own clothes, his own taste in music, there's often a conflict – unnecessarily so.

If we're aware of the illusions that we invest in—even those we hold dearly—we embody the principle of an open mind. We're not trapped by our expectations, nor do we weigh them heavily on others. This principle is what allows us to accept change in our colleagues, as they grow in confidence day to day; to accept them as they adopt behaviours fitting for a responsible and collaborative team player.

With this understanding, we can say that Buddhism itself is an illusion. It's a set of conventions wrapped up as a religion. Buddhists themselves acknowledge that this presents one of the greatest challenges to a monk – overcoming the cultural attachments and preconceptions of what Buddhism is, on their way to achieving enlightenment, whatever that may mean.

In terms of this book and the Learning Grid, it's not so much what's presented, but what's not presented that matters: the gaps between the activities; the space afforded by questions.

For knowledge, add something every day; for wisdom, subtract.
Chinese proverb

Chicken (Leon's version, page 17 – Category: Jokes)

Chicken

There's a whole series of jokes based on the classic "Why did the chicken cross the road?" "To get to the other side" exchange. For example,

"Why did the policeman cross the road?"
"Because it was the chicken's day off."
"Why did Darth Vader cross the road?"

"To get to the dark side."

Come up with two or three new ones of your own, and share them at an upcoming social gathering. Make a note of the insights this activity brings, particularly if they either go down badly or brilliantly. What's important is what you take away from the activity as learning points.

Recommended Kagan Structures:

(1) **To capture thoughts, ideas or questions individual participants may have:** Solo, Solo Pen (an original variation) or Jot Thoughts. (2) **To generate ideas, discuss potential approaches, come up with possible solutions, coach/praise**: 4S Brainstorming, StandUp–HandUp–PairUp (with RallyRobin or Timed Pair Share). (3) **To share:** StandUp–HandUp–PairUp (with RallyRobin or Timed Pair Share) or Inside-Outside Circle. For further ideas, use Think-Pair-Share or see Structure Sequences.[34]

Closed Puzzle (Collaboration Grid, page 41)

A title for a generic type of game which I've used to encourage listening. If the attention breaks down, you get a lot of repetition. If this happens, move on! It only works if enough people buy into the enjoyment of trying to work it out.

The puzzler poses a few statements which minimally describe a scenario in their head, and it's for everyone else to work out what the full scenario is, which is usually rather peculiar. Once the scenario's been set, only yes/no questions are allowed.

It isn't wise to give the answer to these away in any format. It's best to play these games through discovery. One example is, "A man's found dead in a field, naked, clutching a straw. What happened?" The answer's deliberately not been included in this book, so you can derive pleasure from encountering it, with others, in a social context.

Conceptual Triangulation (David's version, page 34)

A thought experiment, in which a few words attempt to triangulate a new concept.

You may be more familiar with this technique as tabloid titles:

- Homeless man under house arrest.
- Students cook and serve grandparents.
- Werewolves sank *Titanic*.
- Siberia melting disaster.

Oriental characters lend themselves to this kind of conceptual triangulation. Examine these lines by Mencius, a famous interpreter of Confucius, which are set out in triads:

人之初 (rén zhī chū) People at birth
性本善 (xìng běn shàn) Are naturally good (kind)
性相近 (xìng xiāng jìn) Their natures are similar
習相遠 (xí xiāng yuǎn) (But) Their habits become different.

The first triad consists of ren (man, person, people), zhi (him, her, it) and chu (at first, basic, junior, beginning), which—juxtaposed—has the meaning 'a person at birth' or 'people at birth'.[35]

Try the following. Contemplate each set, then compare them to what comes up in a Google search:

- postmodernism, Buddhism, civilisation.
- neuron, tribe, event.
- strategy, collective, migration.
- ecological, economics, protocols.

What emerges for you as a result?

Csiklets (Collaboration Grid, page 41)

A theory by Csíkszentmihályi to describe the optimum learning state of 'flow'.

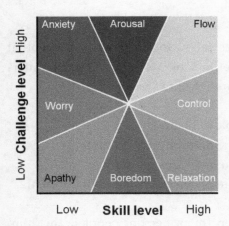

Too hard, students get frustrated or anxious; too easy and they become bored. In order to progress, a perfect path of challenge is needed, matched to the skill set of the students. We're adapting this model in this workshop – not only to participants' individual learning states, but to the whole group as a collective.

How do we go about increasing, or decreasing, the level of challenge? There will always be some participants in the group who enjoy the activity – let them lead. Explanations coming from their peer group have a different effect than those that come from an established 'expert' source.

For example, the participants may come up with a simpler/harder related activity, and given time, this may serve the group well.

Deep Reading (David's version, page 34)

A term to describe a Buddhist practice. In the West, we're used to reading a lot of material. Some pride themselves in the size of their libraries. Some Eastern traditions have a different take on this. They tend to minimise. Could this be related to oriental characters rather than Western alphabets?

Imagine a monk who's studied his mind for a lifetime. He's spent most of his time sitting in front of a wall. Just sitting. Silently. Just before he dies, he writes something, and then he is no more. What do the other monks think of this? How do they approach this text? This one and only expression of a lifetime of mental inquiry?

Buddhists treat such texts as gems. A few precious lines are passed down through the generations. Young monks must prove their capacity before they're given such gems. On a shallow and busy mind, such gems are wasted; so they're preserved, secreted away; revealed only when the monk has the capacity or the potential to understand them. For the gems to be appreciated; for the words to reveal the beauty, the depth of mind of the person reading the text; the experience is less to do with the written words, and far more with how those words are read.

Here's an example text much revered in some Tibetan Buddhist traditions. It's called *The Six Vajra Verses*,[36] or *The Cuckoo of the State of Presence*. Witness how your mind deals with the words for the first time – how resonant, vibrant, or clear; or how dull, lifeless, or opaque. Read them again. Take your time. Close your eyes and reflect on them. Let your mind mull them over, as if you were holding up a gem in the light. Let your mind's eye catch their brightness.

Be the writing. Let your mind take its shape. This is deep reading.

> *The nature of all phenomena is non-dual, but each one, its own*
> *   state, is beyond the limits of the mind.*
> *There is no concept that can define the condition of what is, but*
> *   vision nevertheless manifests.*
> *All is good.*
> *Everything has already been accomplished.*
> *And so, having overcome the sickness of effort, one finds oneself in*
> *   the self-perfected state.*
> *This is contemplation.*

Of course, it's almost impossible to read almost any Western book in this manner. In fact, we're encouraged to read faster and faster, and whole books can be read in a matter of hours. Nevertheless, if you come across something written in this book that strikes you, take time out to appreciate it. Sit back, feel the full resonance of it, let it take mind-shape fully.

Doctor (Leon's version, page 17 – Category: Jokes)

Doctor

There's a whole series of jokes that start, "Doctor, doctor..." A couple of these are:

"Doctor, doctor, what do I need for ingrowing toenails?"

"Ingrowing toes."

"Doctor, doctor, I keep feeling I'm a bell."

"Well, give me a ring when you feel better."

Come up with a couple of new ones on your own and share them at an upcoming social gathering. Make a note of the insights this activity brings – particularly if they either go down badly, or brilliantly. What's important is what you take away from the activity as learning points.

Recommended Kagan Structures:

(1) **To capture thoughts, ideas or questions individual participants may have:** Solo, Solo Pen (an original variation) or Jot Thoughts. (2) **To generate ideas, discuss potential approaches, come up with possible solutions, coach/praise:** 4S Brainstorming, StandUp–HandUp–PairUp (with RallyRobin or Timed Pair Share). (3) **To share:** StandUp–HandUp–PairUp (with RallyRobin or Timed Pair Share) or Inside-Outside Circle. For further ideas, use Think-Pair-Share or see Structure Sequences.[37]

Dream (Leon's version, page 17 – Category: Quotations)

Get a pen and paper ready. First, spend 30 seconds thinking about dreams and dreaming, then write down everything you know about the topics as fast as you can. Take as long as you need to complete the task. When you think you've reached rock bottom, stick with it. Trust me, there's more. (1)

Next, compose some elegant quotations based on your original thoughts. (2)

Stage three is to look up some quotes on the subjects of dreams and dreaming, and see how these ideas compare to yours. (3)

What did you learn? (4)

And now, a final question for you: What did the quotes you found inspire you to say about dreams and dreaming in general and about your own dreams in particular? (5)

Recommended Kagan Structures:

(1) **Individually:** Solo, then Think-Pair-Share or Think-Pen-Pair-Share (an original variation); **in teams:** GiveOne–GetOne. (2) Solo, then Pairs Compare, then share in teams. Assign roles for a Team-2-Team share, eg Amazing Announcer, Super Speaker, Expert Evaluator, Cheerleader – the last handing over to the Amazing Announcer for the next team. Teams swap. The Speaker can either share all four team members' quotes or teams can take turns, with team members rotating roles for another three rounds. (3) Homework, library-based or Internet-based research task individually or in pairs. Share results using RoundRobin or RallyRobin. Teams can then choose the best to share with the rest

of the class using Team Statements or Blackboard Share. (4, 5) Individually assessed statements.

Education (Leon's version, page 17 – Category: Quotations)

Education

Get a pen and paper ready. First, spend 30 seconds thinking about education, teaching, learning, enlightenment; then write down everything you know about the topics as fast as you can. Take as long as you need to complete the task. When you think you've reached rock bottom, stick with it. Trust me, there's more. (1)

Next, compose some elegant quotations based on your original thoughts. (2)

Finally, look up some quotes on the subjects and see how these ideas compare to yours. (3)

What did you learn? (4)

Recommended Kagan Structures:

(1) **Individually:** Solo, then Think-Pair-Share or Think-Pen-Pair-Share (an original variation); **in teams:** GiveOne–GetOne. (2) Solo, then Pairs Compare, then share in teams. Assign roles for a Team-2-Team share, eg Amazing Announcer, Super Speaker, Expert Evaluator, Cheerleader – the last handing over to the Amazing Announcer for the next team. Teams swap. The Speaker can either share all four team members' quotes or teams can take turns, with team members rotating roles for another three rounds. (3) Homework, library-based or Internet-based research task individually or in pairs. Share results using RoundRobin or

RallyRobin. Teams can then choose the best to share with the rest of the class using Team Statements or Blackboard Share. (4) Individually assessed statements.

Elephant (Leon's version, page 17 – Category: Jokes)

Elephant

How do you know an elephant's been in your fridge? How do you shoot a purple elephant? How do you shoot a pink elephant?

Do any of these sound familiar? Why elephant jokes? Don't ask me, but they're a definite genre of humour. Why did I choose these in particular? Because they appeal to my sense of humour! The task here is to engage with them – find as many as you can, tell them, and culminate in a grand finale of composing two or three of your own that make people laugh. If you don't succeed at first, ask yourself, "How did I fail?" and work on improving.

Oh, and by the way, the answers to the jokes that started off this task can be found on page 182.

Recommended Kagan Structures:
(1) **To capture thoughts, ideas or questions individual students may have:** Solo, Solo Pen (an original variation) or Jot Thoughts.
(2) **To generate ideas, discuss potential approaches, come up with possible solutions, coach/praise:** 4S Brainstorming, StandUp–HandUp–PairUp (with RallyRobin or Timed Pair Share). (3) **To share:** StandUp–HandUp–PairUp (with RallyRobin or Timed Pair Share) or Inside-Outside Circle. For further ideas, use Think-Pair-Share or see Structure Sequences.[38]

Explanation (Collaboration Grid, page 41)

See Collaboration Grid walk-through on page 41.

Like an **Introduction** to the Learning Grid, but with more theory. There may be a defined outcome, explaining the purpose of the Learning Grid experience, and the intended objectives.

In the case of the Collaboration Grid, it's the ability of participants to find the qualities required for collaboration to emerge. It's not about defining collaboration, or breaking it down to following simple steps; but encouraging it with activities, and then attempting to locate the qualities within people's experience that enabled it. That is, not objectifying a bullet point of what makes good collaboration, but becoming sensitive to embodied feeling, and states of mind which enable good collaboration.

Because we're approaching collaboration experientially, participants leave with their learning embodied. Participants have a higher chance of implementing their learning directly in new situations, rather than following a mental list of things they should be doing. Also, they can recollect activities at leisure, or a memory of an activity may be triggered in quite a different setting. This gives participants another chance to connect what may appear to be different activities, thus fulfilling the central educational aim of the Learning Grid: synthetic thinking.

Eye-Test (David's version, page 34)

Eye-Test

Which eye do you tend to look out of?

Have you noticed this before? Have you noticed this in others, or in yourself?

I noticed the experience relatively early in life – in my twenties. I realised that I predominantly looked out of one eye. I then wondered which eye people looked through.

I still catch myself looking at actors on screen, watching where their eyes focus while they're talking. I feel we do this when we meet others, and focus our eyes. Which eye do you tend to look at? Do you have a preference for right or left? Might your subconscious actually be trying to catch which eye the other person is looking out of?

I hadn't thought of this for a while; but the other day, this line of thinking resurfaced in a slightly different context. Conduct the following experiment, and see if the following makes sense to you.

First, look at an object in your field of vision, somewhere up ahead and comfortably within range. While looking at the same object, attempt to see it from either eye. Jump—as it were—from looking at the object through your right eye, then your left. In order to help you do this, you can cover up one eye then the other, and if the perspective jumps slightly, you know the eye you have just covered up is the eye you were looking through. Do this enough until you know which eye you're looking through, and you can jump from eye to eye at will.

Next, close your eyes, and do the jumping trick from eye to eye. Be sure not to actually move the eye. It is purely a perceptual jump. Because you have no way of telling from a change in perspective if you are managing this, make sure you can do this. Return to the previous stage if you need to practise more. Once you can do this with your eyes closed, ask yourself the following question:

What's moving?

We're not looking for a definition as an answer. The question's simply attempting to tighten our awareness on what we're actually doing while performing this activity. Whatever your answer is, the more you get to know it, make sense of it, root to it, the easier it will be when we examine what we do with it.

I may refer to it as attention. It might be what mystics have called the third eye – I don't know. What I do know, is that I have this experience. As with most things explored in this way, I return to it over the years with a slightly different angle – more awareness perhaps, informed by more knowledge and more mundane everyday living. I don't expect a definitive answer. The exploration is interesting enough.

So, let me leave you with a third part, something highly speculative, and something I look forward to getting more precision on the next time my mind visits this experience.

Consider the dimension that's moved along with this internal perceptual movement between the eyes. It's horizontal. What then constitutes a vertical dimension? When we move our perception up and down, in what medium is this, internally and psychological speaking? Remember, this isn't a physical movement—neither left nor right in our first experiment—and thus, nor are we moving our eye or any other part of us up and down. What vertical dimension is this?

To my sensibilities, it's a movement up into mind and down into body, but you may have a different take on it. And we can extend this into thinking about the z-axis, forwards and back. And again, if it isn't a physical dimension we're talking about, what might this axis constitute in a subjective and psychological sense? My sense is movement in time.

How significant is it in terms of our communication, or our internal psychology, or even in the origination and formation of mathematics?

I look forward to hearing what others think about what it reveals about our internal lives.

Fingers (Leon's version, page 17 — Category: Riddles)

Fingers

Brows furrowed, thin brown hair tussled, specks of paint on his face and arms; a man in his mid-thirties stands at the top of a wooden scaffold that's ten—no, eleven—men high. He's holding a palette in his left hand, and a paintbrush in his right. He's painting the details on the image of two people's hands; index fingers stretched out towards each other, almost touching. The left-hand figure is that of a man lying on the ground, leaning on one elbow, his left forearm supported on his bent knee. On the right, an older man, clothed in a pink robe floating in a red cloak hanging in mid-air—which also shelters other figures—stretches out his right hand towards the figure on the ground. The sounds of a Catholic mass being celebrated rise up from below. As he paints, he thinks that although what he really wants to do is sculpt these figures in marble—not paint them on a curved surface like this—he's done a good job making sure the figures look realistic when people look at them from floor level.

Who's the artist? And what's he painting?

Recommended Kagan Structures:
(1) **To capture thoughts, ideas or questions participants may have:** Jot Thoughts. (2a) **To generate further ideas and discussion:** Think-Pair-Share, Think-Pen-Pair-Share (an original variation) or StandUp–HandUp–PairUp (with RallyRobin or Timed Pair Share). (2b) **To promote group discussion and solution:** RoundRobin, Single RoundRobin, Talking Chips, One Stray, Travelling Heads Together, leading to Team-Pair-Solo. (3) The activity could develop into a project which could be shared via Poems for Two Voices, Pair Statements, Carousel Feedback, Carousel Discuss, Number Group Presentation, Team-2-Team. For further ideas, see Structure Sequences.[39]

Fool (Leon's version, page 17 – Category: Quotations)

Get a pen and paper ready. First, spend 30 seconds thinking about fools and foolishness, then write down everything you know about the topics as fast as you can. Take as long as you need to complete the task. When you think you've reached rock bottom, stick with it. Trust me, there's more. (1)

Next, compose some elegant quotations based on your original thoughts. (2)

Finally, look up some quotes on the subjects of fools and foolishness and see how these ideas compare to yours. (3)

What did you learn? (4)

Recommended Kagan Structures:
(1) **Individually:** Solo, then Think-Pair-Share or Think-Pen-Pair-Share (an original variation); **in teams:** GiveOne–GetOne. (2)

Solo, then Pairs Compare, then share in teams. Assign roles for a Team-2-Team share, eg Amazing Announcer, Super Speaker, Expert Evaluator, Cheerleader – the last handing over to the Amazing Announcer for the next team. Teams swap. The Speaker can either share all four team members' quotes or teams can take turns, with team members rotating roles for another three rounds. (3) Homework, library-based or Internet-based research task individually or in pairs. Share results using RoundRobin or RallyRobin. Teams can then choose the best to share with the rest of the class using Team Statements or Blackboard Share. (4) Individually assessed statements.

Fox Chick Grain (Leon's version, page 17 – Category: Puzzles)

A farmer needs to get a fox, a chicken and a bag of grain across a river. His boat will only carry a maximum of two items at once, one of which has to be him – who else will row the boat? If he leaves the fox with the chicken, the fox will eat the chicken; if he leaves the chicken with the grain, the chicken will eat the grain. How can he get all three safely across to the other side?

Recommended Kagan Structures
(1) **To capture thoughts, ideas or questions participants may have:** Jot Thoughts. (2) **To generate further ideas and discussion:** Think-Pair-Share, Think-Pen-Pair-Share (an original variation) or StandUp–HandUp–PairUp (with RallyRobin or Timed Pair Share). (3) **To promote group discussion and solution:** Numbered Heads Together or Travelling Heads Together. The

results could be shared via Team Stand-N-Share, Team Statements or Blackboard Share. For further ideas, see Structure Sequences.[40]

Helium Stick (Collaboration Grid, page 41)

A superb way to improve sensitivity and increase teamwork.

Gather a group of four to eight participants to demonstrate the marvellous invention of the helium stick. The participants are asked to put their index fingers out so that the stick rests on all of the fingers (sixteen if there are eight participants). You may have to press down on the stick to make sure there is contact initially.

The objective is to lower the stick to the ground.

The only rule is that fingers must remain in contact with the stick.

As soon as participants are ready, unpress the stick and watch how it magically begins to rise, despite the intentions of all the individuals. Once the laughter dies down, let the groups try or just stick with the same demonstration group.

How do Questions Work? (David's version, page 34)

Rather than having category terms for different types of

questions, might it be useful to know how a question impacts the mind presently, subjectively speaking?

That is a leading question, in that it has a direction.

Consider the quality of the following questions:

- What's the capital of France?
- How do you parse a string in HTML?
- What do I have in my pocket?
- Do cats think?
- What's the answer to this question?
- Am I lying?

What's the difference between pointing at things one knows and pointing in directions one doesn't know? The second type opens up the mind to exploration, and puts questioners in the state of learners.

What seems common to the question-answer pairing is the temporal dimension – that the answer's elicited from the question.

There are specific sets of questions which attempt to disrupt this natural order. They may appear unnatural, illogical or nonsensical, and yet are believed by some to perform a specific function.

The Zen master, Hakuin, is reported to have come up with such a question – a type of koan: *What's the sound of one hand clapping?*

We don't have to chase after the answer of a question, like a dog chasing after a thrown stick.

Inspirationally (David's version, page 34)

Inspiration-
ally

Inspiration's something we're courting with our Learning Grid, but it's a dangerous thing to be too direct about. Inspiration must be approached obliquely. We need to sneak up on it, so that it can jump out at us all of a sudden!

From my experience, playing with inspiration, it's not something which is contained in a person. Although we may feel inspiration—an elation, a lifting—it's a mistake to locate it within the mind, or the body. A classic mistake I experienced while learning to teach was kids attributing the inspiration to me. In their excitement, they'd think I was the source of inspiration; but I soon found that after a short honeymoon period, the magic would wear off, and the contempt that comes with familiarity would set in.

I thus evolved a practice I call 'folding back', where I correctly attribute the location of the inspiration which is in the behaviour, the insight, the genius – in the class. Again, it's not about attributing inspiration to a particular student, but to each person's contribution as it improves the state of the class. It's a thing between. This, I found to be sustainable.

It's something I've had difficulty explaining to adults, and without direct experience, it's nigh on impossible. Many more capable minds than mine have gone to some lengths to describe this, such as Mark Turner, in his use of the term, 'collective cognitive organ',[41] and much of Vygotsky's stance, as exemplified in this excerpt from one of his works:

The experience of the [participant], his emotions, appear not as
functions of his personal mental life, but as a phenomenon that has
an objective, social sense and significance...[42]

I'm an experiential learner. I choose to have an embodied
experience, rather than a verbal description. Hence, this collaboration workshop is a perfect opportunity—as are Learning Grids
in general—for participants to witness how inspiration works
during the course; to its 'location' in the social body, and the
support network; so they can eventually learn to realise it among
their colleagues, and directly with their classes or employees.

The danger of asking for inspiration directly is that it is often
a performance rather than true inspiration which is evoked. All
nice and good at the time to be entertained by some persuasive
and eloquent presenter, but ultimately this doesn't carry through
to everyday experience. Such workshops are considered things of
entertainment or information, and a diversion from normal day-
to-day practice. It's my belief that ordinary day-to-day living can
be quite exceptional, and teachers have the added privilege and
honour of working with people who feel this more than adults.

Whatever the context of our Learning Grid—whether educational or corporate—we're interested in playing in the space of
Not Knowing, a good place to look for inspiration.

How can you apply this in your facilitation of an Odyssey
journey?

Intention Not Expectation (David's version, page 34)

What are your expectations for reading this book? What do you hope to achieve?

What was your intention in taking the reader's journey? What are your intentions at this moment while you read?

Most of us are familiar with expectations – what's expected of us, a standard of behaviour, an objective result to achieve. Intention is more subtle, and a little trickier to put our finger on.

Intention's something within the individual – not obvious, but the source of action or thought. We might be able to intuit what another person's intention was, and we can certainly tell when some social result rolls out that wasn't our intention.

Wouldn't it be useful for us to have a better appreciation of intention, in order to mitigate the sometimes damaging effect that expectations have on us? Perhaps if we have children, adolescents, or we teach – could the appreciation of intention help us avoid the conflict that often arises out of expectations?

If intention and expectation are likened to an arrow, the expectation is the head of the arrow – and indeed, the target of that arrowhead. Intention is the fletching, and by implication, from where the arrow comes. In archery, the head of the arrow against the bow can be moved up and down and side to side. But if the head is held steady, the bow held out forcefully and locked, then we're free to alter the base of the arrow minutely, as it touches the cheek.

Think of any social interaction. What are the intentions of the players? Whatever the expressions, whatever their objectives, what are their original intentions? How close to the heart, their core, are they? Can we take the social risk of asking? Can we apply our skills of communication to reveal our motivations and intentions?

Perhaps this increased appreciation of intention could allow us to align to one another faster, enter into stable trust relationships, enable us to achieve objectives socially.

In the Learning Grid, as a guide, I'm more interested in the interaction of intentions than in the argument of expectations. If our intentions align, then we've a better chance of hitting our mutual targets.

What are your intentions in reading this book? And what's your intention in taking this non-linear path through the material?

Give yourself a chance to consider this. Make a note of it. Return to it when you complete your journey.

Introduction (David's version, page 34)

A general introduction to David's version of the Learning Grid.

Start at the top.

The rule is that participants can choose an activity below an activity that's already been chosen.

Contrast this with **Explanation** and **Opportunity**.

Inventing Equations (Algebra Grid, page 38)

The exercise of turning a situation into an equation. There are two forms of this: interpreting a worded maths problem, and real-world project-based learning.

Provide students with worded equations, such as the example below:

> The cost of hiring seating for the quidditch world cup is 750 sickles per day plus 250 sickles per hour of use. What's the maximum number of hours the seating can be used each day if the rental cost is not to exceed 2,500 sickles per day?

There are plenty of resources available to teachers in schools on the net.[43] Demonstrate how to extract the appropriate mathematical information to create an equation, and then solve it.

The interesting thing about this kind of mental exercise is that it's as artificial as solving ready-made equations. It's an extension of what students have started to learn to do, which is to turn a complex equation into a simple solution; similarly, they must take a complex English language formulation, and reduce it to a simple equation.

Does this suggest, then, that language is simply a more complex form of mathematics? Or that mathematics is simply a minimal language?

Additionally, the formation of equations from a real-world situation can be conducted through project work. A general problem's set, and it's up to the students to work out ways of solving it. For example, how long would it take to fill an 18-wheel tanker using water drawn from a tap?

The methodology is to map reality. The first step's usually determining some form of measurement. Perhaps data can be gathered by measuring how much is filled in a minute of running the tap, and the rough volume of the tanker worked out by estimating the volume of a similar-sized cylinder.

Such physical experiments are relatively simple to comprehend. But further explorations can be suggested by examining the history of science – how Newton managed to mathematise physics in the first place.

But what if teachers posed more abstract questions that haven't been mathematically modelled? What's the equation for love? And how does this differ from love at first sight? Could we produce an equation of how well a class goes? What are the aspects we need to set as variables?

Jokes (Leon's version, page 17 – Category: Conclusion)

Here are three questions for you to think deeply about:

- What did you learn from making and telling jokes?
- What are your favourite types of jokes and How can you tell them better?
- What can you do to make people laugh more often? (1)

What's the next opportunity you have to use these insights in action? (2)

Make sure you use the opportunity, note down what you learned from it, and share it with others. (3)

Where will this take you next? (4)

Recommended Kagan Structures:

Group Investigation or (1) Think-Pair-Share, Think-Pen-Pair-Share (an original variation), or Think-Write-RoundRobin. (2) **In teams:** Simultaneous RoundTable, Jot Thoughts, agree action and follow up with (3) Pairs Compare, Roving Reporter, GiveOne–GetOne. Share results using Team Up! or Team Statements, in which the best four or eight ideas generated are shared from each team, one or two by each team member, to the rest of the class in Team-2-Team or Team Stand-N-Share. (4) Individually assessed statements.

Juggling (Collaboration Grid, page 41)

Using juggling as a physical example of **Simultaneous Processes**, both mentally and socially.

How do you go about showing someone how to juggle with three balls? Do you teach them to juggle two balls in one hand? Do you get them to throw a ball from one hand to the other repeatedly, and then combine two then three?

There's an emergent level of juggling, when it just works. It's obvious when it does. It seems it's only in the last few hundred years that it's stopped being considered a magic trick.

Lateral Thinking (David's version, page 34)

Possibly the most famous of de Bono's inventions,[44] having become part of popular vernacular – also known as the Plus-Minus-Interesting (PMI) tool in de Bono's CoRT lessons,[45] or in other areas as abduction (not deduction or induction), JOOTS, or jumping out of the system. I was lucky enough to hear de Bono talk to a small gathering once, where participants were given several provocative statements, from which they should think 'outside the box', such as landing a plane upside down.

The objective—as always—is less to do with the specific content of a specific thought experiment, but to become familiar with looking elsewhere for the solution to a problem. Thus, when we face traditional problems – eg how to find funding, other solutions are looked for. In order to do this, a common technique is to place ourselves in a situation that's patently absurd; and see what the mind does, as it tries to make sense of it.

Let's contrast de Bono's term of lateral thinking with the subjective experience of one's thoughts, and the impossibility of exact repetition. For example, in the retelling of a story, a different thought comes to mind altering the telling. In fact, it becomes obvious that it's very difficult to cut out lateral thinking. Observe children – it could be said that our modus operandi is lateral thinking, and we require much training to constitute linear thinking.

An entertaining way to exercise lateral thinking is to conduct **Closed Puzzles**, which can be found on various places on the Internet by searching for 'lateral thinking puzzles'. For example:

A man walks into a bar and asks for a drink. The bartender pulls out a gun and points it at him. The man says, "Thank you," and walks out.

The answer's deliberately not been included in this book, so you can derive pleasure from encountering it, with others, in a social context.

Letterbox Protocol (Collaboration Grid, page 41)

Participants are allowed to say only one sentence at a time, and end each sentence in a way that invites others to continue.

A curiously simple technique, that gives rise to a completely different social dynamic. It's not about demanding attention, or trying to say as much as possible in your short allocated time slot.

Listening intensity tends to increase.

Living Wild (David's version, page 34)

Most people are motivated to 'save the planet' in some way. We're aware of the harm we're doing to it. We all try to do what we can, and some of us devote our lives to environmental issues. And those of us with children often feel a strong responsibility to pass on a healthy planet.

But how much can we really be motivated if we spend most of our lives in cities? Or if when we do leave them, we visit rural areas that have been transformed by industrial-scale agriculture? How deeply motivated can we be if we haven't actually experienced the wild – immersed ourselves in the full glory of nature? Is there a relationship between proximity with nature, and motivation to do something about protecting it?

What's the longest period of time you've lived as close to the wild as is possible in our day and age?

Lose Me, We Win (Collaboration Grid, page 41)

While explaining strategy and game theory to a class, I may introduce the boxes game to show how giving away a section of the board turns out to be a winning strategy.

To play boxes, create a grid of dots – say five by four. Opponents take it in turn to draw a line between dots orthogonally (vertically or horizontally not diagonally), using different coloured markers. If by drawing a line a unit box is complete, the player initialises that box and plays again. The objective is to win as many boxes as possible.

The equivalent psychological condition to giving away territory—which goes against the objective of the game—is for an individual to give up their ego, to pull less to themselves when they don't like something, so that others who do enjoy the activity are allowed to, hence the motto, 'Lose me, we win!'.

This strategy works in a cross-disciplinary context, since it enables the more extroverted to 'park' their enthusiasm when they're participating in an activity they don't particularly enjoy. In this way, we have emergent leaders – people leading through enjoyment. Incidentally, this is one of the best ways for someone who dislikes something to get an insight into a subject or topic – through a colleague's enthusiasm.

Boxes is a precursor to one of the oldest and deepest strategy games known to man, GO. It provides an optimal place to become aware of how individual moves can affect groups, and the overall shape of a collective. It's a powerful reflective tool for strategic collaboration.

Map (David's version, page 34)

Map the Terrain – draw an allegorical map of the individual terrain you've travelled as a result of interacting with this Odyssey Grid. Reflect on what you've learned as a result of the journey, and of doing this activity.

Maps (Leon's version, page 17 – Category: Riddles)

Maps

We're in the throne room of a Moorish palace. The room's high walls are richly decorated from top to bottom with bands of colourful interlacing lines and repeated geometric patterns. It's a warm day. The calming sounds of birds chirping, and water falling gently from a central fountain into a long rectangular pool outside, permeate the room. Servants usher in a man. He enters, carrying a bundle of maps and artefacts. He's tall; in his forties. His eyes are lively; he's wearing a smart, long, plain brown tunic, a short brown cloak and a black and silver cross hanging from a silver chain around his neck. He kneels at the feet of a royal couple in an attitude of humble nobility. When told to rise, he does so slowly, with dignity. They start to talk. During the conversation, he rolls out a map, and points westwards to where the wide, empty ocean sea is shown on it. The king and queen listen. She seems more interested in the cross he's wearing than in what he's saying. It's taken him six years of negotiation to get to this point – scholars have looked over his plans before and shaken their heads.

Who's the man with the maps? Who's he talking to? What do they think of his plan? And why does the queen seem more interested in the cross the man wears around his neck than the ideas he's been talking to them about?

Recommended Kagan Structures:

(1) **To capture thoughts, ideas or questions students may have:**

Jot Thoughts. (2) **To generate further ideas and discussion:** Think-Pair-Share (or Think-Pen-Pair-Share, an original variation), StandUp–HandUp–PairUp (with RallyRobin or Timed Pair Share). (3) **To promote group discussion and solution:** RoundRobin, Single RoundRobin, Talking Chips, One Stray, Travelling Heads Together, leading to Team-Pair-Solo. (4) The activity could develop into a project which could be shared via Poems for Two Voices, Pair Statements, Carousel Feedback, Carousel Discuss, Number Group Presentation or Team-2-Team. For further ideas, see Structure Sequences.[46]

Mind Reading (Algebra Grid, page 38)

Discreetly approach a member of the group without the rest of the class knowing – between classes say. Someone who deserves the attention, and also is capable of fulfilling the procedure. Explain the game to them.

At some point during a lesson, a volunteer will be asked for; this person will volunteer, be chosen, and then asked to leave the room. Those in the room choose an object in the room quietly, and the person is asked to return to the room, and guess what object was chosen. Miraculously they choose the object! They must be a mind-reader!

This is how it works. When the 'mind-reader' is asked to return, the facilitator names random objects in the room, to which the mind-reader will respond negatively. At some point, the facilitator will point at an object that's black, and the mind-reader will again respond negatively, knowing that the very next object the facilitator indicates will be the object the group chose.

The objective isn't just to have a laugh, but for the class to try to work out what the rule is. They may begin suggesting experiments – not speaking, for example, just pointing and so on. This collective homing in on a solution is quite a beautiful, creative, scientific and social activity. An aspect of it is like the process of algebra, where a complex equation is simplified until the unknown is revealed.

There are plenty of variations on the rule which triggers the positive response, and it can also be done with pictures, but I don't want to spoil the enjoyment of players discovering these games through participation; the best way to come across them is live.

Mistakes (Leon's version, page 17 – Category: Quotations)

Get a pen and paper ready. First, think about mistakes for 30 seconds, then write down everything you know about mistakes as fast as you can. Take as long as you need to complete the task. When you think you've reached rock bottom, stick with it. Trust me, there's more. (1)

Next, compose some elegant quotations based on your original thoughts. (2)

Finally, look up some quotes on the subject of mistakes and see how these ideas compare to yours. What did you learn? (3)

Recommended Kagan Structures:
(1) **Individually:** Solo, then Think-Pair-Share or Think-Pen-Pair-Share (an original variation); **in teams:** GiveOne–GetOne. (2)

Solo, then Pairs Compare, then share in teams. Assign roles for a Team-2-Team share, eg Amazing Announcer, Super Speaker, Expert Evaluator, Cheerleader – the last handing over to the Amazing Announcer for the next team. Teams swap. The Speaker can either share all four team members' quotes or teams can take turns, with team members rotating roles for another three rounds. (3) Homework, library-based or Internet-based research task individually or in pairs. Share results using RoundRobin or RallyRobin. Teams can then choose the best to share with the rest of the class using Team Statements or Blackboard Share. (4) Individually assessed statements.

Multiple Steps (Algebra Grid, page 38)

A block of equations which involve multiple steps. There are many resources available on the net.[47]

$4x + 3 = 27$

$8x - 5 = 27$

$2x + 9 = 15$

Implementation involves setting strict timings, and 20 minutes is a good amount of time for students to see how far they've progressed – individually and comparatively.

Also, when students ask for help, the guide's job is to remind them of the metaphor they're using. **"On Yer Bike!"** can be a playful, yet affirmative statement, encouraging the student not to lose focus; to keep sight of their target, no matter how fearsome the quarry; just keep aligning their **Arrow And Bow**! Here are some more examples:

$4x + 3x - 2 = 19$

$3(4x - 2) = 30$

$2(6x + 3) + 8(x - 1) = 58$

However complex the equations become in their studies, the three principal processes—as outlined in **Algebra**, framed as a metaphor if required—enable students not to lose track of what they're doing.

Nine Dots (Leon's version, page 17 – Category: Puzzles)

Can you find a way to join all nine dots using three lines, drawn without lifting your pencil or pen from the paper between your starting and ending points? Come to think of it, can you join them all using one line?

Recommended Kagan Structures:

(1) **To capture thoughts, ideas or questions participants may have:** Jot Thoughts. (2) **To generate further ideas and discussion:** Think-Pair-Share, Think-Pen-Pair-Share (an original variation) or StandUp–HandUp–PairUp (with RallyRobin or Timed Pair Share). (3) **To promote group discussion and solution:** Numbered Heads Together or Travelling Heads Together. The results could be shared via Team Stand-N-Share, Team Statements or Blackboard Share. For further ideas, see

Structure Sequences.[48]

Non-Linear Learning (David's version, page 34)

When exploring the activities in these learning grids, how many of your senses are you using? What are your instincts, your imagination, your inspiration tapping into?

The assumption of standard education is that we can provide an objective pathway through the learning material. It doesn't matter what the initial conditions are, who we are, or what we think – we can push people through the same procedure, and they'll come out just the same. Although this might work well for making soldiers and robots, it isn't ideal for nurturing independent thinkers and sensitive learners.

Presenting content in a flexible, non-linear way allows us to welcome serendipity and inspiration into the room. It also allows journeyers to reflect upon the importance of these conditions. There's much more to human engagement than classification. By presenting techniques, games and activities, the Learning Grid contrasts verbal classification with the actual practice of doing, thinking, and reading. We have different modalities of experience, touch, and feelings; previous experience, and future intention. Because of its open-ended nature, the Learning Grid has the potential to take us away from the realm of the symbol, and closer to the realm of the concept/thought symbolised. If conducted with enthusiasm, at the bottom of the grid, you'll be able to review the rate your sensitivity and awareness have improved.

Ultimately, learning's extremely conditional. It depends very much on factors that are out of the trainer's or author's control. There may be a simple exercise, a game that—once played—turns out to trigger a rapid acceleration in understanding – an **Aha!** moment.

Which of the following graphs matches an **Aha!** moment?

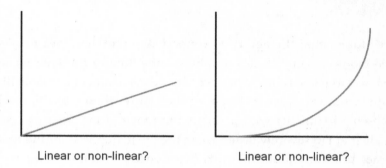

Linear or non-linear?   Linear or non-linear?

The left-side graph is the progress graph we might expect to see in our educational and business statistics. The graph on the right is the kind of graph that start-up businesses like to see, with a rapid take-up of their Internet service. It's also the graph that captures how virals are picked up, with numbers of people increasing exponentially. The left-side graph is called a linear graph because there's a linear relationship between the variables represented on the axes, whereas the variables in the graph on the right have an exponential relationship to one another.

If you don't throw yourself into your own experience, it'll be like evaluating the right-side graph in terms of the left-side graph. And seen in that way, the right-side graph is strangely curved. In terms of nature, however, it's the left-side graph that's odd.

Not Knowing (David's version, page 34)

I've found that the ability to connect different activities breaks the mould of our classical thinking – the kind of thinking we're trained to exercise in our educational establishments. I've facilitated journeys using large grids (more than 10x10), and presented students with a very wide range of experiences – so wide that I'm severely tested when they're juxtaposed for the first time. You'll no doubt find this experience yourself – either as a participant or a facilitator. This kind of synthetic thinking complements nicely the preponderance of 'critical' thinking which we applaud in so many of our Western institutions.

What's the journey we take using an Odyssey Grid; whether in the form of my version, in the form of Leon's, or in the form of any of the variations we have thought of; or even in the form of one of the variations that others are yet to evolve?

At the heart of all these journeys lies social risk; to venture into the unknown; to take a step beyond what we're capable of, beyond what we can predict; to not know what we'll come up with in terms of responses; to celebrate this.

It's a subtle point, the state of not knowing; and too often overlooked. When presented with children who clearly don't know, our natural response is to fill them with knowledge. But it's this state of not knowing—and not the state of knowing, once achieved—which is the source of lifelong learning, which lies at the enigmatic core of curiosity. It's as small and insignificant as the words 'world peace' are grand; as small as DNA, and as wonderful—and inconceivable—as 'life', 'Gaia', or 'God'.

On an Odyssey journey, we typically find we don't know what

comes next; we find ourselves in uncharted waters, where there are no clear, predetermined answers. Why would there be? Do we want to listen to the 'guide' who says they know – full of vision, eloquent in speech; but in the end who doesn't know, or misses out on a facet that could be more rewarding? Or would we rather have someone as a guide who's paradoxically experienced at not knowing? Who, armed with whatever knowledge they may have, is comfortable taking steps into the unknown; so that whatever happens—however surprising, shocking or new— it isn't so much 'knowing' that they fall back on, but the respectful and present-minded response of not knowing, and thus the ability to deal with the present conditions as mindfully and freshly as possible?

Who are these pioneers? We may think of travellers—Marco Polo or Columbus, or the pioneers who travelled across America—whose inner resolve and trust in their own skills equipped them to overcome such hardship. We may think of scientific pioneers like Newton or Einstein making break-throughs beyond the capacity of peers to even contemplate – let alone establish mathematically. But we'd be missing the point.

The truth is, these pioneers are closer at hand. Look at children today. Look how they meet the unknown with courage, curiosity, fear, and thrill. Look at babies, and how they face non-understanding with a smile – and perhaps the innocence of a smile may reveal its true and deep significance in human history, and not as a base mechanical eruption from some complexity of mirror neurons, or any other kind of biological reductionism! The depth of insight of this baby human smiling is rooted purely in the social, and this is where our pioneers exist. The social risk each of us takes on a daily basis remains with us, and defines us now as a conscious species in our time and period, in our history, and potential future. Me writing this right now, and you reading this right now. This is our journey. This is always our journey. We are all pioneers. We all have the potential to be 'confidently unknowing' guides.

What marks out this journey? What 'milestones'? What lightens our load as we travel? What enquickens us?

To become sensitive to new thought. Whether this is within our own being, or—more generously—within another. This is the journey of life. And, should you disagree, look at your grandparents, look at our elders; and see how they delight at their grandchild's learning, their first steps, their first words. To celebrate new learning in others is truly a virtue.

So many of our usual classrooms focus on knowledge accrual and skill development, which provide the bases of most educational theories: Bloom's Taxonomy etc. Developing sensitivity in a complex field of awareness (characterised by higher levels) is a much trickier environment to set up. We need courage. We need self-discipline. We need sensitivity. To be openly vulnerable, to share the journey, whether it's with spotty teenagers in a maths class, or troublesome employees in a company, or even with ourselves sitting alone.

How would you develop this in yourself?

Number Trick (Algebra Grid, page 38)

Ask a student to think of a number between 0 and 10. Have a laugh if they tell you, and ask them again to just think of a number and not tell you.

Ask them to multiply it by 5.

Hold them up one, two or three fingers and ask them to add it to their total. You might want to give the reason for the number, say there are two of you, or there is one light fixture etc.

Ask them to double their answer.

Now comes the really entertaining bit. Lift up both hands and ask a different student to pick a finger, numbering from 1 to 10. Turn away so you can't see which finger they choose. Ask this student to whisper their number to the student who'll add it to their total.

Tell him to reveal their total answer. In a flash, or taking your time, reveal to the student which number they picked, and the finger the second student chose.

Don't explain how this works, but as you progress through the grid, and you do the trick a few times, challenge the students to create an equation to explain how the game works.

The equation before the finger-number is added is $2(5x + 1, 2$ or $3) = 10x + 2, 4$ or 6. So if they state 86, you know their original number was 8, quick as a flash. The point of the speed is to show them that you're not calculating the answer, working back. You're using algebra.

Odyssey (David's version, page 34)

See the Odyssey Section on page 34.

Odyssey
page 34

What comes to mind when we hear this word?

The Odyssey is one of the oldest epic poems in Western literature. Believed to be written by Homer, in ancient Greek, it relates the tale of Odysseus's attempt to return to his homeland of Ithaca, following the Trojan War – a journey that is beset by challenges, adventures and tests of skill, wit and fortitude.

As a result, the word Odyssey has come to mean a long or adventurous journey.

Have we named the book—and the experience of journeying through the Dynamic Learning Grid—well?

On Yer Bike (Algebra Grid, page 38)

On Yer Bike

Ask students how they learned to ride a bike. Evoke as many details as possible – the type of bike, who showed them, perhaps the first day they actually could cycle by themselves without stabilisers. The processes for learning to ride a bike match how they're learning to do algebra.

First, you have to pedal. You pedal one side, then the other. You have to balance out the pedalling; you can't just do one side. You have to pedal one side and the other. In algebra, this is like the equal sign.

Second, you're told to look up. A lot of kids fall over because they're looking at their feet; or they're turning their handlebars, and the bike turns and falls over. The trick is to just look ahead. In algebra, this is having x on one side of the equal sign, and whatever's on the other side as the answer.

Third, you have to turn round corners, otherwise you crash into things or hit a kurb or cycle off the car park. Then you may cycle on different slopes, surfaces, and bumpy terrain, or you end up learning tricks. This is like algebra when you start with something simple, but you end up going over more and more complex terrain, and learning neat tricks.

The most important aspect of the learning experience is the very counter-intuitive action of cycling faster to be safer. If you pedal too slowly, you fall off. It's actually easier to maintain balance on a bike when you pedal faster. But this is risky for the young cyclist. If you can remember, it's rather scary to move on a thing which is balanced on wheels half-an-inch wide. In mathematics, this means applying the three processes (see **Algebra**) with conviction, and... repeat repeat repeat.

And what happens if you fall off your bike? What did those adults say? What did you do? Yup, you got back on your bike, or in Scottish parlance, "On yer bike!" A useful refrain for students when they keep putting up their hands, when they get stuck. Don't help them until they've tried.

Open Puzzle (Collaboration Grid, page 41)

A generic term for a logical deductive word game.

Someone presents a couching scenario, eg "I'm going on a picnic, and for this picnic I am going to take a..." and they name their object. The initiator needs to have a secret rule in their head to which all objects need to conform.

Participants take turns to list objects. The initiator has to say whether they'll be allowed to participate in the picnic – depending on whether their objects conform to the secret rule or not.

The object of the game is for participants to guess the secret rule through a process of deductive reasoning.

A good starting rule is to match the initial letter of the word to the initial of the person. So, Douglas can take his dog to the picnic, but Patricia can't take her dog. Perhaps eventually she finds she can take her parakeet – as well as a pencil, procrastination and any other word that begins with 'p'. Yet another version could be "Behind the green glass door are kittens but no cats." (Can you work out why?)

The rules don't have to be word-related. They could be based on physical actions or gestures while a word's being said.

Other versions are "I can pass through the green glass doors because I'm carrying a…" (the rule being something of the colour that matches something they're wearing), eg if wearing a blue shirt, "carrying a blue box".

The rules are usually very simple, but are sometimes tricky to spot. The dynamic of the game results in some people guessing correctly and thus they have the rule inside their head too, and thus the number of people who don't know gradually reduces.

It's important to note in any kind of puzzle game, the answer should never be divulged! The longer people take to work it out, the more disappointed they'll be upon being given the answer; they must wait it out to the bitter end. It's also interesting to note where a person responds to this experience as "duh! how stupid of me," or flush with satisfaction after finally having worked it out for themselves.

There's also art in giving clues, by choosing words that hint at the rule. People should be careful to give more abstract, lateral clues first. Enjoy!

Opposites (Algebra Grid, page 38)

Opposites

Remind students of the four operations (addition, subtraction, multiplication and division), and challenge them verbally to give you the opposite. For example, +7 has an opposite of -7. Multiplying something by 4 is the opposite of dividing it by 4.

This isn't an exercise in understanding, but an exercise in

training – repetitions at the gym, speed and accuracy. It's usually something students find trivial, but for some there's something enlightening about the simplicity.

The standard method of teaching algebra has been to ensure students know how directed numbers work, how to manipulate negative numbers – and if this is covered beforehand, all well and good. However, the benefit of using an equation is to see why we learn such things. There's a result – a solution to a problem.

There are two ways the guide can run this. One way's not to connect up the activity, and see if the students bring to play this notion of opposites when conducting another activity. Another way's to ask the students what the effect of doing the opposite is; what are the numerical results when calculations involving opposites of addition and subtraction and opposites of multiplication and division are performed?

Opportunity (Leon's version, page 17)

See page 19.

The Page Is Blank (David's version, page 34)

It's quite tricky to see this, because this book's manifest as a complete thing before you. This sentence you're reading now begins with the word, 'This' and ends with the word 'end'. But at the time of writing, the sentence you're now reading began with the word 'But'; the end hadn't been written; and there was merely blank space which was filled with words, to convey some kind of meaning, and ending with a 'point'.

That is, in the writing, the page was blank. Remind yourself by getting a pen and paper, and notice how the page is blank as you write. Notice how each letter comes out, forming words, and the words form phrases, and these constitute sentences...

... and paragraphs.

Can you read with this sensitivity? Can you read as if the next sentence hasn't been written? Of course you can see the next paragraph ahead – you could jump to it now. But the writer's stuck here, in a flow of thought, communicated word by word by word. And if you honour the writer, and wish to follow the line of thought they're taking, of course you won't jump ahead. You'll respect their effort; and take your time, reading each word, each phrase, until we're ready to move on to the next paragraph.

It's tricky to ignore the fact that all the words have been written; and instead, to progress, at the same time as if you were writing each word now – this one, then this one, just as the writer has. If you can do this, you're much more aligned to the writer, where the commas really work as pauses, and... there may even be ellipses to give the matter a little more thought.

Read like this, the page *is* blank. Indeed, the book is empty. Read (past tense) like this, the reading becomes as much a journey as the writing, full of discovery and surprises. And what occurs in your mind is as valid as what happens in the mind of the author.

Does this liven up the material? What do you think?

Pay It Forwards (David's version, page 34)

Catherine Ryan Hyde wrote a book called *Pay It Forward*,[49] which has been made into a film. The premise of the book is that a boy named Steve conducts a social experiment, by performing three acts of kindness. Instead of wanting to be repaid for his generosity of spirit, the rule is that each of his recipients pay the kindness forward to three others. His dream, and the dream of the author, is that it transforms the world.

It's a simple enough idea, and the maths is valid. Why, then, isn't our world replete with these acts of kindness?

Given an opportunity to exercise this, were someone to do a significant act of kindness for you, would you feel impelled to do this for three others?

Principal Methodology (David's version, page 34)

We're interested in the awareness of 'the conditions of thought', the learning environment in our offices and companies and schools. Our primary methodology differs radically in a number of ways:

- **Not Knowing** – do first, then think about it. It is participation, not comparison and judgement for experience and contemplation that comes first;

- social feedback loop – social results, seeing what works, say yes, experimentation, willingness, alignment, consensus, flocking, emergence;
- sensitivity to conditions – within our minds, to others, to the moment of learning, amplifying genuine learning insights, as well as new skills;
- **Simultaneous Processes – Non-Linear Learning**, systems thinking process rather than static, the **Aha!** moment, building concepts, being creative.

In this way, we delve deeper than knowledge, category, or language games; and deeper than skill transference, and technique familiarity. We source our selves more in the current moment, the actual conditions that occur; and we use whatever skills, techniques, knowledge available, to maintain the richest learning environment for the learners in our charge. And our skill, as collaborators, is to provide the right conditions for learning to occur. This happens at many levels of being—motivational, conceptual, physical—all at the same time. This is less static and slow management; and more organisational, present-minded **Juggling**!

We operate in the 'beyond-comfort-zone', alternatively described by Csíkszentmihályi as 'flow' (see **Csiklets**). Too difficult, and participants phase out; too easy, and they get bored. The trick is to find the sweet spot which is challenging enough, but not too challenging. The emphasis is often put on the manager to find this sweet spot for those for whom they're responsible. However, our emphasis is to encourage everyone to ascertain their own level of challenge – and generally this is beyond one's comfort zone. To be comfortable in the space of **Not Knowing**—the state familiar to the learner—contrasts strongly with the notion of the manager, or boss, as expert who may occupy higher positions of authority, and may be an expert of their specialist knowledge field; they may manifest enough wisdom to assist, but they can't pretend to be an expert in terms of another person's learning. And this is no less true for collaboration between peers in a team.

If the methodological shift occurs, the result is a lot of 'learning' and 'collaboration' – so much that it's difficult to control in the traditional sense. At the same time that we, our colleagues, our bosses, are liberated, we need to impose more self-discipline. Each of us becomes responsible for our individual contributions – for our influence and impact upon the collective. Neither is this leadership in the traditional sense, where someone is going to lead everyone to what they presumably need – an underlying belief which underlies a lot of current business practice. The creative act involves **Not Knowing**; it emphasises the phase of getting-to-know, of discovering, of inventing. If this is managed well—again, not in the traditional sense; but in the sense of being sensitive to it and allowing it to be pursued in the genuine sense of adventure and exploration— so our offices, our companies, our schools, our minds, our very lives are transformed.

Push Me Pull You (Collaboration Grid, page 41)

Either to be conducted with an example pair, or done in pairs with everyone.

Pairs are formed, and are asked to hold hands. One is told their objective, which is to touch the chair on one side of the room, the other is told their objective, which is to touch the chair on the other side of the room. Go.

How many pairs struggle in competition? How many competitions are won by the strongest? And how many negotiate, and then take it in turns to walk calmly to one chair then the other?

Puzzles (Leon's version, page 17 – Category: Conclusion)

So you ended up at **Puzzles**. What did you find puzzling about your journey? What did you find clear? What made the puzzling puzzling to you? What made the clear clear to you? Think about these questions for 30 seconds, then write down what your conclusions are as fast as you can. Take as long as you need to complete the task. When you think you've reached rock bottom, stick with it. Trust me, there's more. (1)

By the way, have you ever invented a puzzle? Well, now's your chance – use what you've learned so far in the Odyssey journey you've just taken to try your hand at inventing a puzzle or an enigma which you can then share with others. A new puzzle is a gift, so don't devalue it by telling people the answer too soon. Let them grapple with it for a bit. If they ask you for the answer, give them a clue if you want, but refuse twice before giving them one. The sense of achievement they'll have, if they work out the answer for themselves, before getting a clue—or the answer— will be all the greater. (2)

Recommended Kagan Structures:

Group Investigation or (1) Solo, then Think-Pair-Share, Think-Pen-Pair-Share (an original variation), or Think-Write-RoundRobin. (2) **In teams:** Simultaneous RoundTable, Jot Thoughts, then RallyTable. Share puzzles using Numbered Heads Together.

Quotations (Leon's version, page 17 – Category: Conclusion)

So you ended up at **Quotations**. Quotations, proverbs, sayings: What makes a good quote? What do these traits have in common with the many ideas you encountered on your journey? Think about these questions for 30 seconds, then write down what your conclusions are as fast as you can. Take as long as you need to complete the task. When you think you've reached rock bottom, stick with it. Trust me, there's more. (1)

Next, take at least five to ten minutes to list some proverbs, sayings, or famous quotes. They can be on anything under the sun – from the Bible, Shakespeare, things family members tend to say. If you think you've hit rock bottom, keep going – that's when the good stuff tends to surface. (2)

Do the quotes you've gathered fall into patterns? What makes them stand out? What can you deduce from the ones you've gathered, the ones you've made up and the others you're familiar with? (3)

Recommended Kagan Structures:

Group Investigation or (1) Solo, then Think-Pair-Share, Think-Pen-Pair-Share (an original variation), or Think-Write-RoundRobin. (2) **In teams:** Simultaneous RoundTable, Jot Thoughts, then (3) Pairs Compare, Roving Reporter, GiveOne–GetOne. Share results using Team Up! or Team Statements, in which the best four or eight ideas generated are shared from each team, one or two by each team member, to the rest of the class in Team-2-Team or Team Stand-N-Share.

Riddles (Leon's version, page 17 – Category: Conclusion)

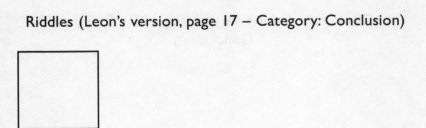

So you ended up at **Riddles**. Where do riddles come from? Where do the answers come from? If you made up a riddle to which you didn't know the answer, would anyone be able to come up with *the* answer? How do your answers relate to the experience you've had of going on your own Odyssey journey? (1)

Have you ever invented a riddle? Well, now's your chance – use what you've learned so far in the Odyssey journey you've just taken to invent a riddle, then share it with others. A new riddle's a gift, so don't devalue it by telling people the answer too soon. Let them grapple with it for a bit. If they ask you for the answer, give them a clue if you want, but refuse twice before giving it to them. The sense of achievement they'll have, if they work out the answer for themselves, will be all the greater. (2)

Recommended Kagan Structures:

(1) **To address questions:** Think-Write-RoundRobin, Jot Thoughts, Think-Write Pairs Compare (an original variation), Numbered Heads Together. (2) **To generate ideas on how to compose riddles from scratch:** Talking Chips, RoundTable Consensus. **To invent riddles:** Group Investigation **OR** (1) Solo, then Think-Pair-Share, Think-Pen-Pair-Share (an original variation), or RallyTable. Get inventors to share their puzzles in pairs using Pairs Compare or Stir-The-Class, or use RoundTable Consensus to get agreement on the best one in each team and share using Blackboard Share then Pairs Compare.

Scouting (Collaboration Grid, page 41)

Scouting

The facilitators mingle with the participants, as if they're one of them.

They get a participant-eye view of the workshop – an invaluable perspective.

In addition, the responsibility of the learning is clearly centred on the group, encouraging them to self-organise from the outset.

The facilitators also get to note the self-starters, those reluctant to take authority, and people with other qualities, which can be fed back to the individuals as well as to the group (without needing to divulge individuals' names).

Shells (Leon's version, page 17 – Category: Riddles)

Shells

Hey! Look out to sea! There's the emperor's trireme – that big ship with the three banks of oars. The trumpeters are getting ready to play a fanfare. Listen! He's probably going to give a speech in a minute. It's nearly 100 years since Caesar landed in Britain and we have a situation. There's fighting in Britain and we're being sent to sort it out. There aren't that many of us and it's been a long, hard march through Germania down to the coast of Gaul. And now, here we are, on the coast of Gaul, being ordered to get the battle gear ready – on the north stretch of the beach, some of the legionaries are checking the stone-throwing machines we call *ballistae*; to the south, others are setting up the large dart-throwing machines we call *catapultae*. But wait. What's that he's saying? He wants us to gather a whole lot of seashells? And why's he dressed like that? Who does he think he is? Venus?

Who is this emperor? Why have the soldiers been asked to gather seashells? And why is he dressed this way?

Recommended Kagan Structures:

(1) **To capture thoughts, ideas or questions students may have:** Jot Thoughts. (2) **To generate further ideas and discussion:** Think-Pair-Share (or Think-Pen-Pair-Share, an original variation), StandUp–HandUp–PairUp (with RallyRobin or Timed Pair Share). (3) **To promote group discussion and solution:** RoundRobin, Single RoundRobin, Talking Chips, One Stray, Travelling Heads Together, leading to Team-Pair-Solo. (4) The activity could develop into a project which could be shared via Poems for Two Voices, Pair Statements, Carousel Feedback, Carousel Discuss, Number Group Presentation or Team-2-Team. For further ideas, see Structure Sequences.[50]

Simultaneous Processes (Collaboration Grid, page 41)

Instead of learning sequentially, one learns simultaneously.

The minimal, non-trivial, system to comprehend contains three elements. A two-element system tends to opposition, dichotomy, argument – A or B. We're interested in a more complex, dynamic system, where initial conditions can produce chaotic behaviour, and for this it's best to use three starting elements.

The trick is, from a whole range of phenomena—eg the field of maths—what are the elements one chooses? These elements are more like principles than topics, or objects of thought; and avoid easy categorisation. Their nature's processual.

Simultaneous Processes is about mentally juggling three or more processes in the mind at the same time. Breaking down the system into its three separate elements destroys the systemic level. Analysis and words have limited use. It's more important that one can do it, rather than describe it.

One of the best ways to represent this is with **Juggling**, once considered magical, which also shows my technique for teaching **Algebra** (see the Algebra Grid on page 38).

Social-Learning (David's version, page 34)

Here's a social experiment: when it occurs to you next, give the person you're with some money – enough for it to be meaningful. Observe their response. They'll probably ask why, but only give as much reason as is necessary – for example, the simple fact you'd like to, or it's part of a gift-it-forwards experiment. Try to be as clean as possible, so there's nothing on your side but the act of giving.

What would happen to you were this to happen? Has this happened to you already? Is this similar to the experience of receiving money from your parents when you were a child?

What's going on for us to think and feel what we do? There are deep insights into our human nature, our sense of identity, our sense of possession and the mechanism of money itself. But rather than theorising, experiment.

Or, if you want a clean and abstract way to learn what the effect of teamwork is, play the computer game Armagetron,[51] a version of snake in teams. Download a client version, find a fortress server (or set one up) and invite your friends (or the participants to the workshop) to a game. Starting in your own zone, your team's objective is to enter the opponent team's zone. The first and most important lesson to learn is to grind centre, to align to teammates, for reasons of offence (to outflank the opponents) and defence (to seal the entrance to your zone). This has been the most graphic and rapid way to demonstrate social learning in my teaching experience.

The Space Between (David's version, page 34; Collaboration Grid, page 41)

Consider this thought experiment. In physics, there's a concept called the centre of weight, or the centre of balance. If we think of a power relationship between two people, is it biased towards one or the other? In terms of the psychological engagement between people, a couple or a team, where's the centre of balance?

By considering this, we escape the notion of discrete beings, and thereby disarm many of the arguments that prevent us reaching peaceful resolution. We can move away from saying people are clever or stupid, or being hurtful. We know that cleverness is a relative measure, and that hurtfulness can be a complex dynamic. By locating the source of these attributes and energies as being in the 'space between', all parties are invited to contribute.

Alternatively, to get an abstract sense of the 'space between', play GO. GO is one of the oldest non-trivial strategy games known to man. It takes a few minutes to learn the rules, but a lifetime to master. Why? Placing stones on a grid's easy enough, we can see them as easily as checkers on a board. What's harder to see is something the Japanese call 勢力 (seiryoku); 外勢 (gaisei), or 'influence' – how the stones interact. Because of the number of permutations, logic and reasoning break down, thus introducing a more intuitive or artistic interpretation. Playing GO—and appreciating influence between stones—can provide a metaphor for understanding the complexities of interaction between people, which I believe is also beyond our capacity to compute.

Subjective Enumeration (David's version, page 34)

Subjective
Enume-
ration

Simply estimate the value of your experience on a scale of 0 to 10.

Once you conduct an activity, let your mind come up with a number. If this is tricky, think of as many factors as possible – from judgement of the experience like it was out there, like the size of the moon; to your most innermost evaluation, in terms of your life's goals; and everything in between. Also consider how receptive you are at the moment – whether you're capable of appreciating it, and so on.

The following levels of separation help me:

- 0 meaning it was completely worthless;
- 1–4 meaning it was good, but nothing actually happened, no tipping point;

- 5–7 excellent, a palpable change of thought, heart, behaviour… actionable;
- 8–9 exceptional, amazing, insightful, transformative;
- 10 invaluable, off the scale, resonant to the point that I knew this already, deeply.

Subjective Enumeration is an interesting exercise that enables you to track your progress through the book, and it may be a starting point for comparing experiences with others.

I invite you to use it to evaluate your experience of engaging with the activities in this book from now on.

Subjective Tests (David's version, page 34)

An external test is something which attempts to measure a student's learning through comparison to a standard – thus, we derive success and failure.

A subjective test is a means by which a person becomes aware of how they perform, through a precise reflective exercise. It's not quite so easy to define what a subjective test is, but let's try to approach it obliquely.

Statistics are used for objective tests, and become redundant for subjective ones. It doesn't matter if 10% of the population is illiterate – it depends on whether a specific person in a specific situation is. One's height can be compared with others', but one's height is just one's height; the same goes for one's knowledge of a subject.

What's worse, is that objective tests measure static quantities – and do very badly with respect to potentials, which are heavily influenced by motivational factors.

So, the difference between an objective and a subjective test is one of perspective. To a teacher who wishes to compare students, the scores are useful. To the specific student who wishes to evaluate how well they are doing, their individual score is useful. It's the same test, the same score. And a good teacher will consider the subjective meaning of a test score relative to the learner.

So, consider school exams, or professional challenges and deadlines. How do you feel about them? Take a moment to reflect on your childhood experiences, because they strongly influence how you may have behaved subsequently.

Did you worry about the exam marks when they were handed out? Perhaps it was because of the relative comparison to friends – where you were in the class order. Or maybe it was simply to find out how well you'd done irrespective of others.

Was your emphasis on the results? Or did it depend on how well you did in the exam itself?

This is a good indicator on the objective/subjective test divide – if the student can tell whether they've done well or not in the actual exam. After all, if you think about it, the results are just a mechanical consequence, a totalling up, a summing up – the real activity was doing the exam.

Is a professional sportsman concerned with being in the first string of the team, getting a place in the finals, with winning? Or are they concerned with performing to the best of their abilities – and if this means they end up on a podium, so be it?

When it comes to more 'external' skills, like throwing a javelin or being able to write a book, competition may play a part. For some people, becoming famous is everything. When it comes to more 'internal' skills, like developing awareness, becoming sensitive to feelings and thoughts of others, competition and comparison is simply inappropriate.

So the question is, are you reading objectively or subjectively? Are you comparing this book to others? My writing to Leon's? Or are you evaluating it relative to your own sensibility?

And from a certain frame of reference – that life is a test – where is your balance?

Substitution (Algebra Grid, page 38)

Substitution

Demonstrate substitution in a formula and provide a block of material for the students. There are many resources available on the net.[52]

Calculate R when $p = 6$, $q = 12$ and $s = 3$

$R = rs$

$R = 4p$

$R = 2r + 2s$

The method of substitution is relatively well understood—in and of itself—though, of course, formulas can get quite complicated. Simply replace each variable with a constant.

I've found that it starts to get tricky when teachers introduce it as a method to check the answer of an equation that has been solved algebraically. Using the Learning Grid, a student may volunteer this method to check their answer, by substituting their derived solution into the original equation, and seeing if both sides are equal. Having the method volunteered by a peer seems to stick in students' minds better.

Sum Equations (Algebra Grid, page 38)

Demonstrate simple addition and subtraction, multiplication and division in equations.

$x + 5 = 12$

$x - 4 = 7$

$3x = 21$

$x/4 = 5$

Provide students with a block of repetitive questions, and give them five minutes to get as far through it as possible.[53] It's a matter of practice, of training. Understanding is the ability to perform the trick.

This level may appear trivial, and many students will find this easy by using the method of trial and error. With such students—indeed, with everyone—the trick is to emphasise the algebraic method. Finding the answer isn't a problem, so fix their attention on the method; use any of the metaphors, or abstract principles, to frame the process of finding a solution, ie balancing, aim, and simplification. In our first equation, we aim for x by itself; to do so, we get rid of the 5 by subtracting 5; if we subtract 5 on one side of the equation, we must take 5 away from the other side.

If done well, students will be able to complete the more complex equations. Those who trust the guide/teacher, and adopt the method, will find harder equations doable; thus justifying to other students the benefit of trusting the guide. Those who don't, will experience difficulties, since the trial and error method has more specific—and perhaps limited—use. However, these students will be able to catch up, if they adopt the algebraic method; and next time the guide/teacher suggests something, they'll all have a shared experience to encourage trust. This sets up a good relationship with the students – one of functional trust, rather than needless authority.

Taking The Stand (David's version, page 34)

Given the level of environmental degradation, what can we do about it?

Many of us have adopted some practices which attempt to mitigate global greenhouse build-up, recycling waste, buying more fuel-efficient cars, shopping locally; but the planet continues to heat up.

Given that the ice caps are melting, who'll be the first to suffer? Should we concern ourselves with their plight before it happens?

There are entire countries which will disappear when the ice caps melt. The Maldives, for example, has a high point of 2.4 metres above sea level currently.

What are they doing about the impending disaster? Are they taking steps to migrate? Can anything be done to help them? Or are these island peoples proactively attempting to halt the melting ice caps? And if so, what can be done to help them?

In terms of climate change, I believe this is the front line. I am taking the stand with the islanders.

Where are you in relation to the peoples of the world, and the environmental disaster to come?

Textango (David's version, page 34)

An interesting reading and writing experiment which subverts our customary, Western way of reading.

Textango is the live editing of a single page document by multiple authors.

It's conducted on line, using a shared interface such as Google Docs.

There are many ways to set the starting point of the textango. A single word in the centre of the screen which may capture the theme, problem, or objective, or one word at the top and one at the bottom, and so on.

The rule of **Textango** is that the writing and reading are limited to a single page.

Let's say two people decide to textango. They decide on a common word, theme, or problem they want to work on. After a while – leaving it a while allows thoughts to drift through their mind subconsciously – they meet on line to textango.

They set up a document showing their common word, a statement of the agreed theme or problem, or each can choose a different word as a springboard to a thought process. They select a piece of music to listen to simultaneously. This sets a time limit for the **Textango** session, and allows non-rational thinking to play a part in the interaction.

As the music plays, they type text, edit, change, retype; their thoughts flowing into each other's and into the on-line document.

It's a difficult thing to describe using the written word, so we've put a video up on YouTube to demonstrate – search for

'David Pinto Leon Conrad Textango'.

An optional ending is for participants to sign the document in the last few seconds of the music track using a means of contact such as a Twitter handle, Facebook link or email.

If there are several writers, the **Textango**'s between them, and sometimes it's tricky to see what they're doing because of the multiple points of attention.

Give it a go. How well does your attention match the other writer's? How is the experience of reading? And how does it differ from standard 'fixed' text, like the text you find in books?

Does **Textango** provide us with a medium by which we can capture certain qualities of thought that elude traditional forms of literature?

Try it and see.

Thank You (David's version, page 34)

Thank
You

Genuinely, thank you for taking a journey through this grid and trying the activities.

I'm currently writing a book about ecological economics, called *The GIFT*, the financial protocols of which are based on giving. In the process of gift-giving, there is gratitude. We have an algorithm that tracks gratitude. I believe this may be a better system than money.

If this book's useful, this may fund further exploration and experiments in ecological economics. So, thank you.

Triple Teams (David's version, page 34)

An advanced team-working technique. Teams are formed in three different ways:

- by ability,
- self-organised or friendship group,
- and optimised teams chosen by the facilitators.

The first is usually done with respect to a task – for example, writing code, or dealing with clients; the second is self-organised, which often follows friendship groupings; the third is usually the choice of the manager, once they become sensitive to types of personality or a simple team system such as Belbin team roles (plant, coordinator, shaper etc). On any given day of group work suited to the activity, groups are organised in one of these three ways. Points are scored throughout the duration of a project. With a good variety of teams, and conducted over a period of time, each individual thus has a number of daily scores from each of their three teams – an individual ranking based on group participation.

For the purposes of this workshop, there is plenty of opportunity to arrange the participants in equivalent categories of subject/interest/ability (eg maths specialists, arts specialists etc), by self-selection, and random. This technique can be used while conducting the team games.

Generally, the following simplified roles are distributed to players:

- Scribe: note-taker, person responsible for anything which is shown to others;
- Timekeeper: not only works within time constraints, but also schedules workflow;
- Chairperson: ensures everyone is accountable, as leader or facilitator;
- Resources Manager: gathers materials, returns them, keeps things tidy;
- Spokesperson: represents the group verbally.

Twittering (Collaboration Grid, page 41)

Simply encourage the participants to share their thinking through tweets.

This may be ongoing while an activity is underway, and is especially valid when listening to a lecture.

Hints on the use of hash tags may also be helpful, so a continuity of conversation can occur.

Txt Wtht Vwls (David's version, page 34)

Is it rlly pssbl tht we cn rd txt tht mts ths nmbr of vwls (whl kpng intct tw-lttr nd sngl-lttr wrds)? It pprs we cn. Wtht vwls in spch, of crs, it wld be mpssbl, bt it lks lke hmn brns thnk in trms of cnsnnts whn we rd. Wld ths wrk if we jst hd vwls nd mttd cnsnnts? I dn't thnk so. So, if ths is wrkng at th lvl of wrds, nd we dn't rd wrd fr wrd, wht is hppnng at sntnc strctr? Hw mny wrds cn we mt in our rdng nd yt rtn an ndrstndng of th ndrlyng mnng?

The original text reads as follows:

> Is it really possible that we can read text that omits this number of vowels (while keeping intact two-letter and single-letter words)? It appears we can. Without vowels in speech, of course, it would be impossible, but it looks like human brains think in terms of consonants when we read. Would this work if we just had vowels and omitted consonants? I don't think so. So, if this is working at the level of words, and we don't read word for word, what is happening at sentence structure? How many words can we omit in our reading and yet retain an understanding of the underlying meaning?

It's interesting to see what the mind's capable of. A similar thing happens with speed-reading.

Most of what we do here is go in the opposite direction. To pay attention to the moment, the continuous revealing of meaning in the act of creation, in the act of writing one letter and word after another, in matching our reading to the writer's experience. There's no objective to rush to, no single overriding conclusion. The Learning Grid is about the journey, within one's own mind, within the community who pursue the 'same' journey.

Types of Meditation (David's version, page 34, Collaboration Grid, page 41)

Meditation isn't exclusively Buddhist, in the same way as reasoning isn't exclusively 'scientific'. The exercise of meditation is to slow down body and emotions, so that one can become aware of sensations and thoughts as they rise and fall away. With practice and courage, this sensitivity carries over into everyday living, whatever the speed or conditions a person finds themselves in. It's about attuning oneself to what is.

There are two main forms of meditation: single-pointed, or focused meditation; and broadening awareness, mindfulness meditation.

A good way to describe these is using the metaphor of our senses – our vision, for example. Consider how we attend to what we actually focus on as it contrasts with how we attend to things in our visual field without actually looking at them.

There's also an opportunity to go into how Buddhists approach the voidness of things, using point meditation and negation. They focus their mind on an object – say this book. The mind will wander from it – where this specific copy of the book came from, or the language in which it's written, or the history of the Gutenberg press, or the origination of capturing language with a script, or the technology of pulping wood to make paper, or the art of calligraphy, and so on. Each time the mind goes wandering off on an associative path, it's returned to this thing in your hands and it's reaffirmed mentally that whatever was thought about was not this actual thing but a thought. Each and every path away from this thing is reaffirmed as a thought-path, and not the actual thing.

If this mental experiment is conducted so that every possible path away from this thing in your hands is traced and negated, whatever is left is the thing on its own. Buddhists call this process emptying, or appreciating the voidness of a thing. And once they master this for a thing, they turn it upon themselves, and perform a similar emptying process upon what the self is.

The softer approach is the art of mindfulness. This involves softening the focus of attention, expanding it to take in more sensory input at the same time, which is more closely related to an unfolding, like a lotus flower – slowly becoming aware of all that is. This gradual releasing of one's grip of mind allows the person meditating to sink deeper into their body, which is why it's sometimes termed heart meditation. It's associated with the path of peace, tranquillity, loving-kindness.

For the purposes of your journey through this book, even a taste of meditation may provide you with some sensitivity to your own mental processes – not taking the process of reading for granted, becoming aware of the incredible processes involved in learning. Try either of these techniques – whether by yourself, or by attending a local meditation gathering. Either way, it involves zazen (literally seated meditation) or sitting – just sitting, pure sitting, and nothing but sitting.

Typewriter (Leon's version, page 17 – Category: Riddles)

Type-
writer

It's a Friday evening in May 1917. We're in the Théâtre du Châtelet in Paris. The ballet we've just seen—if that's what you can call it—has lasted around 15 chaotic minutes, during which we've been assaulted by dancers pretending to be part of a group of street-performing circus artists: a Chinese vaudeville magician, a girl in a sailor suit, a pair of jugglers, a strange pantomime horse, and a couple of managers dressed in 10-foot-tall costumes made of cardboard and papier mâché they can hardly move in, extending the characters' forms into space in all directions; our ears battered by the sounds of an orchestra amplified by typewriters clattering away, whistles blowing, foghorns booming; our eyes lambasted by a set with buildings going off at all angles, with no sense of perspective whatsoever. As the curtain goes down, there's a riot – boos, hisses break out all round. Women, brandishing their hatpins like weapons, go for the artists, wanting to gouge out their eyes. I know it's wartime, and these Russians are known for their strange work. But still! And yet, what else can explain the last quarter of an hour?

What's the work that's just been performed? Who do you think the composer, set designer, and choreographer might have been?

Recommended Kagan Structures:

(1) **To capture thoughts, ideas or questions students may have:** Jot Thoughts. (2) **To generate further ideas and discussion:** Think-Pair-Share (or Think-Pen-Pair-Share, an original variation), StandUp–HandUp–PairUp (with RallyRobin or Timed Pair Share). (3) **To promote group discussion and solution:** RoundRobin, Single RoundRobin, Talking Chips, One Stray, Travelling Heads Together, leading to Team-Pair-Solo. (4) The activity could develop into a project which could be shared via Poems for Two Voices, Pair Statements, Carousel Feedback, Carousel Discuss, Number Group Presentation or Team-2-Team. For further ideas, see Structure Sequences.[54]

Unlearning (David's version, page 34)

You're probably familiar with 'Don't think of a giraffe'. The mind can't help but think of a giraffe, it seems, even if it doesn't enter our primary attention as an image.

This goes for all our associations. Once we've learned something, it's very hard for us not to follow the lessons we've learned. The older we get, the more ingrained we become in our behaviour patterns; the more we attach ourselves to specific tastes, specific behaviours – so we become dated, old.

Unlearning is the process through which we negate such learning, not just replace one learning with another. This happens naturally as we age – as energy reduces, so the effort to maintain certain behavioural patterns dwindles. If we're careful about it, we can let those aspects of us that are foolish drop off first. A side effect is that we may appear wiser.

Look back at the second paragraph. Is it really true that 'it's very hard' for us not to follow the lessons we've learned? Perhaps we should use a different metaphor, it's 'tricky' rather than 'hard'? And once we've learned the trick, to shift metaphor, it's easy.

One persistent lesson to which we constantly seem to fall prey is the use of the present tense when describing processes that are malleable: "We get trapped in the present tense." Whereas, we could say, "We got trapped in language," or "Language trapped us," adopting the past tense in order to provide us with a little more flexibility in our present condition.

The Chinese only have one verb form, which—if unmodified—denotes the present tense. Could this be one of the factors that has led to the persistence of their social institutions?

Unlearning is the softer version of scepticism. It's not about not trusting our teachers, our language, or our institutions; it's about letting go of those processes and practices that are contained in repeating behavioural patterns that are neither helpful to ourselves nor to others. It's not simply that we're critical, but that we question the source of these processes and behaviours...

... so that when someone mentions a giraffe, we pay less attention to the giraffes that might arise in the mind, and more to why they're talking about giraffes in the first place.

Why are we talking about giraffes?

Unstuck (Collaboration Grid, page 41)

A procedure to employ when engaging someone who thinks they're stuck.

This just means their mind can only see one way of doing something, or they are caught in a loop of reasoning they can't escape from.

Invite a participant up, demonstrate the procedure with them, then invite participants to pair up and lead their partner through it.

First, get your partner to explain the loop, the dead end they are in, genuinely. The trick in listening is to avoid negating this problem, and try to clarify it by adding to the detail. This curiosity in what the mental situation is normally results in a state of confusion. Increase and dramatise this. This may become comical, how the mental state turns in on itself quite often, how it brings in other completely unrelated phenomena.

Because the partner has appreciated your genuine listening — and when they hear their mental anguish explained, they distance themselves from it—it's no longer stuckness, but confusion – a mess.

Then, at the high point of confusion, take a step back into your own reality, and state a simple description about the subject matter – your simple way of seeing something. When your partner returns to the material, they can't help but see the simple way of approaching it.

Being unstuck usually releases the energy that was caught in the stuck state, which makes tutoring or therapy an enlightening experience.

A word from the wise: kids know a good thing when they experience it. They don't look back when they encounter a simple thing. Adults, on the other hand, have a tendency to be amazed for a few minutes, and then say, "But it wasn't this simple before…" and subsequently go looking for their stuck state. That is, adults are often attached to their stuckness – it's become part of their identity. The remedy is simply for the adult to want the new unstuck understanding more than their old sense of identity. So, to start, ask your partner how much they'd like to get rid of this stuckness, and then hold them to it.

Warning (David's version, page 34)

Warning

What you're about to experience has a style and nature to it that pushes against—and indeed breaks through—the boundaries between reader and writer, between words and thoughts, knowledge and awareness.

I'm a postmodern journeyman, a bricoleur through and through. I'm aware of my environment, mentally, and I make use of what's around me. Often I find myself using the concepts and beliefs other people carry around in their heads. This serves me well in the real world, in classrooms, and business meetings; but not in the written word, for I don't know what you think or feel. And since I'm more concerned with how and why you think or feel, rather than what you specifically think or feel, it leaves us with a quandary: How do I go about writing this?

I have concerns that the material may be too complex, the conceptual jumps too wide, the narrative continuity not rich enough with metaphor. Will we get to the point at which we'll have experienced enough, done enough activities, that I may ask for greater patience from you, the reader? I hope we do.

So, with this intention, I've provided activities that are challenging in their own way. They provide a means of 'training' – though really it is about disarming critical thinking, sidestepping the mind's capacity to categorise and then link up words linearly—logos and logic—so it's less training, and more unlearning; more being, and less doing.

And, if you look down at the bottom of the grid, you'll see that **Unlearning** is one of the topics – so I'm getting ahead of myself here.

I've apologised. I've intimated the direction of our journey ahead, but—so far—this doesn't constitute anything close to a warning. Warnings imply danger, so does this mean danger lies ahead? Well, only insofar as approaching the experience of reading may upturn certain assumptions, some of which may be deeply held. This can turn out to be quite challenging.

And here's the benefit of a book – you may go at the pace that you choose. If you find the material in this grid too challenging, try Leon's on page 17. For out of the greatest challenges come great insight, and great resilience; and I very much look forward to hearing what your mind and heart come up with.

Be well!

What Do You See? (David's version, page 34; Collaboration Grid, page 41)

Try this thought experiment – it's not a logical one, or something which requires reasoning. It's more like inviting you to be sensitive to your mind.

Take a few moments—a minute, at least—to think about what you see below:

When you've done this, turn to page 174 to explore this further.

What Is Money? (Collaboration Grid, page 41)

This may seem out of keeping with the rest of the material in the

Collaboration Grid, but I believe it underlies why we live in a competitive society, rather than a collaborative one. Remember that the point of the Learning Grid is for the guide to share what they believe is important; to show vulnerability, to share what they think, so the journey through the Learning Grid becomes a journey of mutual sharing and deepening. It's in this spirit that I offer up this activity.

Invite the participants to examine the current axioms of current economics:

- A pen for a £1 coin or a dollar bill – *money as a form of exchange*.
- The £1 coin or dollar bill is later exchanged for an ice cream – *money as a store of value*.
- The pen and the ice cream can be enumerated on the same scale – *money as a unit of account*.

Firstly, by emphasising the mundane point of exchange—the pen for the £1 coin or dollar bill—we obfuscate the singular purpose of giving. The coin or bill and the pen aren't for one another, but *for the people involved*: the pen's for the person to write with, and the £1 coin or dollar bill is for the ice cream a little later. Thus, an 'exchange' is an instance of mutual giving, a snapshot. We'd never confuse a photo for real life, but we regularly confuse money for a real thing.

Secondly, by relying on money as a store of value—the £1 coin or dollar bill carrying value between the pen and the ice cream—we overlook the actual fluidity of value. A '£1 note' used to be exchangeable at the bank for one pound in weight of silver; in 1785 a silver standard was set for the dollar. At the time of writing, £1 buys 0.05 ounces of silver; a dollar 1.14 grammes. Modern money has sublimated from a thing (its weight in silver) to an abstract number game (relative exchange rates of currency), so that even the £1 coin or dollar bill we received for the pen isn't the same £1 coin or dollar bill we give for the ice cream. We misperceive money to be a stable storage of value.

Thirdly, by using a singular unit of account, if both the pen and the ice cream are worth £1/$1, we risk losing the quality of our experience. If we can conflate the use of a pen or the taste of an ice cream to a single dimension, can we conflate all our human values—our aspirations to become better people, our love for our children, our appreciation of nature, or even god—to a single dimension of enumeration?

Then introduce a different financial protocol that is based on collaboration:[55]

David wants to invite Annemie for a week. At the start of the week, both David and Annemie bring their £1,000 (or $1,500 – the equivalent for a week's time) and agree on the two conditions of the social contract. First, that the direction of the money is towards Annemie; David guarantees his £1,000/$1,500 will be released to Annemie at the end of the week, in effect doubling her money. Second, whatever is co-created is non-owned, so that whatever money is attracted is divided equally between them. Throughout the week, while producing their pitch or participating in a workshop, David and Annemie (and anyone else for that matter) enumerate their ongoing experience; their equal share is distributed by the weightings they have set individually (tracked with a variation of Google's PageRank algorithm). Ideally, David is paying Annemie for what she wants to do, rather than our normal contract of employment, which is to do what the employer wants.

What's the difference in feeling when we are paid to provide a service, rather than invited to co-create? How might this shift our work patterns? Could such a new financial protocol shift us from a competitive culture to a collaborative one?

When's Tea? (Collaboration Grid, page 41)

A little information on the expected schedule of events during the workshop: break, lunch etc – just so participants have a sense of the parameters of the workshop.

Where's The Verb? (Algebra Grid, page 38)

Observe the following equation, which a child would probably treat with familiarity:

3 + 2 = 5

Here's the thought experiment:

Where's the action in this simple sum? Where's the doing bit? Circle the bit of that 'sentence' that is the 'verb'.

Take a moment to be sensitive to how your mind thinks of it, otherwise the subtlety of the next section may be lost.

Now turn to page 174 to explore this further.

Who Chooses? (Collaboration Grid, page 41)

What are the possible ways for the group to make a collective decision about how to choose the next activity?

An obvious way is for the guide to pass the choice to a volunteer, and once that volunteer chooses an activity, to pass on the power to a person of their choice. It makes sense to pass this on, so every person in the group gets a chance to pick an activity.

Out of interest, can a group make a unanimous decision simultaneously? What are the conditions that are needed to allow that kind of behaviour to emerge? Hypnosis and autosuggestion aside, can you think of ways you might facilitate this?

Wisdom (David's version, page 34)

Here's the definition in the New World Encyclopedia, at the time of writing:

> *Wisdom is a type of knowledge, similar to phronesis, that includes judgment for its proper applications to a given situation. The status of wisdom as a virtue is recognized in various cultural, philosophical, and religious traditions.*
>
> *Most psychologists regard wisdom as distinct from the cognitive abilities measured by standardized intelligence tests. As such, in*

general, wisdom is determined by one's ideals and principles that govern all actions and decisions. Applications of personal wisdom include one's ethical and social guidelines in life that determines one's unique personality, short and long-term goal(s) pursued in life (spiritual or materialistic for example), perspective on life, and social attitudes.

I personally take wisdom as a function of awareness and action. It's embodied intelligence. It's not objective, but subjective. There are variations in the sayings and actions of wise people, and this depends on the level of awareness their action is grounded in – whether it's at the level of co-existence with all living things (Buddhist), all human beings (humanist), or some small political grouping (most theorists and politically wise individuals).

So, the question is, does the Learning Grid enable an exploration of wisdom, rather than the simple dry investigation and training of the intellect?

Wording (David's version, page 34)

This is a little tricky to perform, since we're constrained by the written word in our communication here. Try reading the following passage to a friend or partner, and see what their experience is, or have them read it to you. Feel free to extemporise to get the most out of the experience.

We tend to think that we speak words. This is an illusion brought about because of our preponderance on the written word. Something about what I am doing right now has been translated into little scrawls and scribblings as letters, blocked into words, with gaps between them. But there are no scribblings in my speaking right now. And can you actually tell if there are gaps between words?

Listening carefully, there are no such things as gaps between words. There are pauses, and these are captured in English with punctuation. But on the whole, it has a 'sing-song' quality to it. Perhaps I can speak some foreign language at this moment so that you can really hear the continuous sing-song quality of wording?

So, if it isn't words I'm speaking, and I'm simply wording, wording, wording, then does this give us an alternative understanding of meaning? And might this suggest that computer scientists are going about it the wrong way; trying to finding meaning in words, when evidently, there are no words? Meaning from wording may provide a more fruitful approach.

And if this isn't enough, consider the following statement from the I Ching (or Book of Changes):

Writing cannot express wording completely.
Wording cannot express thoughts completely.
Are we then unable to see the thoughts of the holy sages?[56]

Wrong, Wrong, Right (Leon's version, page 17 – Category: Puzzles)

How can two wrongs make a right? See if you can work it out.

Recommended Kagan Structures:

(1) **To capture thoughts, ideas or questions participants may have:** Jot Thoughts. (2) **To generate further ideas and discussion:** Think-Pair-Share, Think-Pen-Pair-Share (an original variation) or StandUp–HandUp–PairUp (with RallyRobin or Timed Pair Share). (3) **To promote group discussion and solution:** Numbered Heads Together or Travelling Heads Together. The results could be shared via Team Stand-N-Share, Team Statements or Blackboard Share. For further ideas, see Structure Sequences.[57]

What Do You See? – Commentary

I've conducted this experiment with my students, and their answers indicate the predilection of mind for different forms of thinking.

Some see a letter 'h', or 'b', or the digit 6, which indicate an imaginative turn of mind – even more so for those who see a house, factory, chair, or even an upside-down flag. A plainer description might be five dots or five black dots, which is going some way to a scientific bent of mind. Some see the relationship or alignment, describing a square and a triangle. They're all valid, of course, once pointed out.

Where's The Verb? – Commentary

When asked where the action is in this equation, most people say it's in the 3 + 2 part, where the adding occurs. We can understand this in terms of time, where we start with three things and we add another two things, which is true of course. However, there's another way of looking at this sentence.

Imagine you're looking at a bowl of fruit. There are three apples and two bananas in it. We can either see the three apples and two bananas OR we see the five pieces of fruit. That is, the action of the mind is in the equal sign – we're either holding 3 + 2 in our mind, or we're holding the 5. Relate this to the two hemispheres of the brain, parts and whole, analysis and synthesis. Relate this to Bertrand Russell's theory of classes. This simple sum becomes the minimal sentence that contains the basic property of classes in language – that is, three apples, and two bananas; or five pieces of fruit; as well as capturing the mind's ability to see two different ways of seeing the same thing.

So, there are two ways of looking at even a simple sum. Conduct this experiment with students, and observe the results. Both are valid. The question is, is this an insight into our root way of perceiving and understanding? And if so, how does this influence how we see the rest of the world?

It is valid, therefore, to appreciate that further—more abstract and complex, mathematical concepts—may possess alternative ways of understanding. Subsequently, the received understanding that teachers are familiar with may not be the only way of understanding. This opens up the potential for teachers to learn alternative forms of thinking. And what better way for this to occur than from listening to students who perceive an alternative understanding 'naturally'?

Bibliography

Books

de Bono, E, *De Bono's Thinking Course*, BBC Books, London, UK, 1982/95.

de Bono, E, *The Use of Lateral Thinking*, Penguin Books, Middlesex, England, 1982.

Boyer, CB (Ed), *A History of Mathematics* (Second Edition), John Wiley & Sons, Inc., NY, USA, 1991.

Csíkszentmihályi, M, *Flow: The Psychology of Happiness: The Classic Work on How to Achieve Happiness*, Rider, London, UK, 2002.

Doidge, N, *The Brain that Changes Itself: Stories of Personal Triumph from the Frontiers of Brain Science*, Penguin, London, UK, 2008.

Dweck, CS, *Mindset: The New Psychology of Success*, Random House, London, UK, 2006.

Dweck, CS, *Mindset: How You Can Fulfil Your Potential*, Robinson Publishing, London, UK, 2012.

Gray, D; Brown, S; Macanufo, J, *Gamestorming: A Playbook for Innovators, Rulebreakers, and Changemakers*, O'Reilly Media, Inc., Sebastopol, CA, USA, 2010.

Grove, DK and Panzer, BI, *Resolving Traumatic Memories: Metaphors and Symbols in Psychotherapy*, Irvington Publishers, Inc., New York, NY, USA, 1989.

Haven, K, *Story Proof: The Science Behind the Startling Power of Story*, Libraries Unlimited, Westport, CT, USA, 2004.

Hebb, DO, *The Organization of Behavior*, Wiley and Sons, NY, USA, 1949, republished by Taylor and Francis, 2009.

Jacobs, J, *English Fairy Tales*, David Nutt, London, UK, 1890.

Kagan, M; Kagan, L and Kagan, S, *Classbuilding: Cooperative Learning Structures*, Kagan Publishing, San Clemente, CA, 2012.

Kagan, S and Kagan, M, *Kagan Cooperative Learning*, Kagan

Publishing, San Clemente, CA, 2009.

Kagan, S and Kagan, M, *Teambuilding*, Kagan Publishing, San Clemente, CA, 2001.

Kagan, S; Kyle, P and Scott, S, *Win-Win Discipline*, Kagan Publishing, San Clemente, CA, 2004.

Lawley, J and Tompkins, P, *Metaphors in Mind: Transformation through Symbolic Modelling*, Developing Company Press, London, UK, 2000.

Marzano, R; Pickering, D and Pollock, J, *Classroom Instruction That Works*, ASCD, Alexandria, VA, USA, 2001.

McCracken, J, *Clean Language in the Classroom*, Crown House Publishing, Carmarthen, UK, 2013.

Michels, M, *Cooperative Learning and Science*, Kagan Publishing, San Clemente, CA, 2003.

Norbu, N, *Dzogchen: The Self-Perfected State*, Arkana Penguin Books, London, UK, 1989.

Pirsig, R, *Zen and the Art of Motorcycle Maintenance*, Vintage, London, UK, 2004.

Pinto, D, *Educare*, Lulu, Raleigh, NC, 2008.

Ruskin, J, *Mornings in Florence*, Homewood Publishing Company, Chicago, USA, 1895.

Santarcangeli, P, *Il Libro dei Labirinti: Storia di un mito e di un simbolo*, Sperling & Kupfer editori, Milan, Italy, 2000.

Sullivan, W and Rees, J, *Clean Language: Revealing Metaphors and Opening Minds*, Crown House Publishing, Carmarthen, UK, 2008.

Tims, C (Ed) et al, *Born Creative*, Demos, London, 2010.

Turner, M, *The Artful Mind: Cognitive Science and the Riddle of Human Creativity*, Oxford University Press, Oxford, 2006.

Wilhelm, R and Baynes, CF (Translators), *The I Ching or Book of Changes*, Bollingen Series XIX, Princeton University Press, 27/1997.

Articles

Brefczynski-Lewis, JA; Lutz, A; Schaefer, HS; Levinson, DB and Davidson, RJ, "Neural correlates of attentional expertise in long-term meditation practitioners" in *Proceedings of the National Academy of Sciences*, 104 (pp 11483–11488), 2007.

Dent-Brown, K, "The Six Part Story Method (6PSM) as an aid in the assessment of personality disorder", in *Dramatherapy*, Vol 21, Issue 2 (pp 10–14). Routledge, London, UK, 1999.

Dolci, D, "The maieutic approach: the plan of a new educational centre at Partinico" in *Prospects: Unesco Quarterly Review of Education*, Vol 3, No 2, Unesco, Paris, France, Summer 1973.

Feller, RJ and Lotter, CR, "Teaching Strategies that Hook Classroom Learners", in *Oceanograpy*, Vol 22, No 1 (pp 234–237). Rockville, MD, 2009.

Lahad, M, "Storymaking: An assessment method for coping with stress". In Jennings, S (Ed), *Dramatherapy: Theory and Practice 2* (pp 150–163). Routledge, London, UK, 1992.

Lahad, M and Ayalon, O, "BASIC Ph: The Story of Coping Resources", *Community Stress Prevention* (Vol II), Kiryat Shmona, Community Stress Prevention Centre, Israel, 1997.

Vygotsky, LS, "On the Problem of the Psychology of the Actor's Creative Work", in *The Collected Works of LS Vygotsky* (Vol 6: Scientific Legacy) (R Rieber, Ed.; MJ Hall, Trans., pp 237–244). Plenum, NY, USA, 1999.

Digital resources

(All links tested and confirmed functional at time of printing; *denotes a site related specifically to mathematics.)

Anon, *Positive Interdependence, Individual Accountability, Promotive Interaction: Three Pillars of Cooperative Learning*, Foundation Coalition brochure, no date. Available on line at the Foundation Coalition website – www.foundationcoalition.org/publications/brochures/acl_piiapi.pdf

* Centre for Innovation in Mathematics Teaching website – www.cimt.plymouth.ac.uk

Foundation Coalition website (in particular the section on Collaborative learning) – www.foundationcoalition.org

Kagan Online website – www.KaganOnline.com

* Kuta Software free worksheet generator – http://www.kuta software.com

* Manga High website – http://www.mangahigh.com

* Math.com website – www.math.com

* Math-Drills.com website – www.math-drills.com

* Mathematical Association of America website – www.maa.org

* The Maths Zone website – www.themathszone.com

McCracken, J, *Boosting Children's Thinking Skills – and Stopping Playground Fights,* Podcast interview with Judy Rees, April 2012 (Podcast). Podcast link: www.box.com/s/38cd66162 cf1acf4dc99

Panitz, T, "A Definition of Collaborative vs Cooperative Learning", in *Deliberations* on the London Metropolitan University website, 1996 – www.londonmet.ac.uk/delibera tions/collaborative-learning/panitz-paper.cfm available at http://ccti.colfinder.org/sites/default/files/a_definition_of_col laborative_vs_cooperative_learning.pdf - TinyURL: tinyurl. com/Panitz-01

Peter Dahmen – Graphic Designer and Paper Artist – www.peter-dahmen.de – www.popupkarten.de

Stahl, RJ, "Using 'Think-Time' and 'Wait-Time' Skilfully in the Classroom", *ERIC Digest,* Bloomington, IN, May 1994 – www. ericdigests.org/1995-1/think.htm

Walker, C, *Clean Questions and Metaphor Models,* TEDx Merseyside Talk, 4 February 2012. YouTube link: http:// youtu.be/aVvcU5gG4KU

Walker, C, *Caitlin Walker Presents an Introduction to Clean Language and Systemic Modelling,* iDevelop, no date (DVD)

Walker, C, *Using Clean Language to Resolve Conflicts and Boost*

Results In Education, Podcast interview with Judy Rees, February 2012 (Podcast). Podcast link: www.box.com/s/u21q duvr31g6nrds2vxo

Wenger, W, *Project Renaissance* website – http://www.win wenger.com

X-ray Listening website – www.xraylistening.com/blog/2012/ 04/16/boosting-childrens-thinking-skills-and-stopping-playground-fights

Yellow Bridge website – www.yellowbridge.com

Resources

Remember – the most powerful resource you have will always be the creative potential of the people in the room, but specific tools (and Odyssey Grids are a prime example) are sometimes needed to focus that potential, so here are some additional tools you might find useful.

On our website at www.odysseygrids.com, you can find a range of resources, including:

- Templates for Odyssey Grids in printable format,
- Templates for Odyssey Grids in on-screen format,
- Activity Cards for hosting an **Action Cycle,**
- **Textango** demonstration,
- And much more.

For maths and other on-line resources, see the list within the Bibliography on page 178.

Answers

Elephant

"How do you know an elephant's been in your fridge?"

"Footprints in the butter."

"How do you shoot a purple elephant?"

"With a purple elephant gun."

"How do you shoot a pink elephant?"

"First you paint it purple, then you shoot it with a purple elephant gun."

B&W

The miller's daughter picks a stone out of the bag and immediately drops it. "Oh, I'm so sorry," she says. "How clumsy of me! But wait – if I've picked out the black stone, the white one must be in the bag. If there's a black stone in the bag, I must have picked the white one." The landlord's reaction went unrecorded, but he kept his word; and the next harvest was such a good one, they managed to save up enough money never to get into arrears with the rent again.

Explore something that interests you about this riddle that you didn't know before. Identify as many significant things as you can that you learned as a result of engaging with the puzzle.

Fingers

The artist is Michelangelo. The picture is his *Creation of Adam* on the ceiling of the Sistine Chapel in Rome.

Explore something that interests you that's related to this riddle that you didn't know before. Identify as many significant things as you can that you learned as a result of engaging with this topic.

The Fox, the Chicken and the Grain

The farmer takes the chicken over, leaving the fox and the grain together. He comes back alone and takes the fox over, returning with the chicken. He leaves the chicken back on the first side of the river and takes the grain over, returning to pick up the chicken. It takes seven trips, but he manages to get all of them over to the other side of the river safe and sound.

Explore something that interests you that's related to this riddle that you didn't know before. Identify as many significant things as you can that you learned as a result of engaging with this topic.

Maps

The man with the maps is Christopher Columbus. He's talking to Queen Isabella and King Ferdinand of Spain. They're sceptical of his plan; but after taking advice, as they have some surplus money, they decide to give Columbus the benefit of the doubt, and speculate. Queen Isabella's as keen to bring more souls into the care of the Catholic Church as she is for Spain to be able to discover a new route to get to the east coast of India, to make trading easier.

Explore something that interests you about this riddle that you didn't know before. Identify as many significant things as you can that you learned as a result of engaging with the topic.

Nine Dots

The three lines can extend well beyond the 3x3 grid and don't have to pass through the centres of the dots:

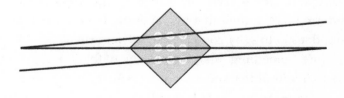

The dots can be joined with a single line in two ways:

1. cut the grid into three lines, lay them side by side and draw a line through them:

(well, no one said you couldn't!), or

2. use a thick line:

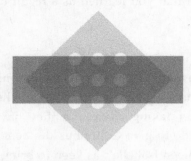

(it's just a question of thinking differently).

Identify as many significant things as you can that you learned as a result of engaging with the puzzle.

Shells

The emperor's the Roman emperor Caligula – one of the more eccentric of the emperors of Rome, if not the most eccentric. He's decided to gather his army on the coast of Gaul to invade Britain, but the invasion never happens. He's asked the soldiers to gather seashells to take back to Rome as tribute, to allow him to claim he's conquered the sea. He's dressed as the goddess Venus – well, considering he's argued that his favourite horse should be made consul, doesn't this, by comparison, seem normal?

Explore something that interests you that's related to this riddle that you didn't know before. Identify as many significant things as you can that you learned as a result of engaging with this topic.

Typewriter

The scene describes the première of the ballet, *Parade*, composed by Erik Satie, with a set designed by Pablo Picasso, and choreography by Léonide Massine, produced by Sergei Diaghilev and performed by his *Ballets Russes*. The ballet was based on a scenario by Jean Cocteau. Apart from being infamous for the reaction it produced, the performance also produced the first written reference to surrealism in the programme notes written by the French poet Guillaume Apollinaire.

Explore something that interests you about this riddle that you didn't know before. Identify as many significant things as you can that you learned as a result of engaging with the topic.

Wrong, Wrong, Right

Two wrongs *can* make a right if you think of them mathematically. There are a number of solutions. One is shown below.

```
  W  R  O  N  G        4  9  2  6  5
+ W  R  O  N  G      + 4  9  2  6  5
_____   _____
  R  I  G  H  T        9  8  5  3  0
```

See if you can work out a couple more.

How many significant things that you've learned as a result of engaging with this puzzle can you list and describe? Why are they significant to you?

Forthcoming titles in the Treasure Trove series of Cultural Riddles

Riddles From History

Over 25 well-known scenes from history presented as riddles suitable for use with Odyssey boards. Each riddle is presented with an enticing title, a set of clues, a detailed historical essay outlining the facts and context in which the events take place, and a list of cross-curricula activities that could lead out from an exploration of the subject.

A sample of a riddle and clues is shown below:

G

My face has been shaped with a metal file; my shoulder grooved; my foot nicked. My face has been covered in soot to see what I look like in mirror image. I've been thrust into red hot flames to harden me; plunged into a bucket of water to temper me. I've sired many offspring that form groups and families to make powerful marks wherever people use them. I'm small, but powerful. So powerful I've changed the world.

I started off in the Far East, but revolutionised European history when I was recreated by a German goldsmith, entrepreneur and inventor in Mainz.

What am I? Who was this German goldsmith who recreated me? And what are we most famous for?

Clues

1 The goldsmith's surname began with G.
2 It happened in the 1440s.
3 A vital factor in the success of this invention was that the first paper mill in Germany was opened in the 1390s.
4 Another vital factor in the success of this invention was the creation of a thick, oil-based ink.

5   The goldsmith went into this as a plan 'B' when investors who had wanted him to make concave metal mirrors to catch miraculous rays from relics that were exhibited to pilgrims every four years were thwarted when the pilgrimage for the following year was cancelled due to an outbreak of the plague. To get some return on their money, they decided to invest in this idea instead.

6   The patronage of the Catholic Church helped get this idea off the ground.

7   The invention was later instrumental in supporting the establishment of the Protestant Church.

Riddles From Art

Over 25 well-known scenes from the history of art presented as riddles suitable for use with Odyssey boards. Each riddle is presented with an enticing title, a set of clues, a detailed historical essay outlining the facts and context in which the events take place, and a list of cross-curricula activities that could lead out from an exploration of the subject.

:)

Sunlight streaming through tall windows on one side of this room reveals that it could belong equally to an artist, an architect or an inventor. The first thing it meets is a desk, on which are laid out charcoal pencils, quill pens and an ink pot, and an open notebook with detailed sketches of machines and human figures annotated in a small, curly hand which is quite difficult to read. Further on, a tall, handsome man in his late 50s, with a flowing mane of hair and a long beard, plainly dressed in the garb of an artisan is standing by an easel, talking to a younger man, roughly 30 years his junior, richly – no, regally – dressed. They are quietly, yet earnestly discussing the picture on the easel: a picture of a woman with an enigmatic smile. Their shadows fall on a globe and stretch from Italy to France. Can you name either of the two men? What is the painting they are talking about? What signifi-cance do the shadows have?

Clues

1 He was known as a polymath (he was a painter, sculptor, model maker, set designer, metalworker, mechanical and structural engineer, architect, musician, scientist, mathe-matician, inventor, anatomist, geologist, cartographer, botanist, writer and philosopher) – he's probably the most famous polymath in the world.

2 This meeting is likely to have happened in Bologna, in Italy.

3 The older man had just made a mechanical lion as a centre-piece for an important meeting that the younger man had had with the Pope.

4 The conversation resulted in the older man moving to France, where he spent the rest of his life where he was put up in a castle which you can still visit today.

5 The younger man was King Francis I of France.

Riddles From Bible Stories

Over 25 well-known scenes from biblical stories presented as riddles suitable for use with Odyssey boards. Each riddle is presented with an enticing title, a set of clues, a detailed historical essay outlining the facts and context in which the events take place, and a list of cross-curricula activities that could lead out from an exploration of the subject.

Terrible Twos

Some say it never happened.

Some say it only happened to a few people.

Some say it happened to thousands.

Others... well, they stay silent. The grief is too great to allow them to speak.

For those that hear it, the noise is deafening. The kind of noise that makes your brain spin, your guts turn, your eyes water, your body reel. You're unlikely to hear the like of it, and you'll be thankful for that. Thankful you'll never hear what they hear: the cries of mothers in mourning; the cries of dying children, run through by spears; the cries of fathers dying while trying to save their youngest sons – not one of them over two years old. Some older children are speechless. Some are adding their howls to the general cacophony. One child, probably the same age as you, is curled up in a corner, hugging a dog, finding comfort in the warm fur and the wet tongue, licking the boy's face clean. This was such a nice place before the king ordered the slaughter. Why would he do such a thing? Why here? Why now?

Where is this scene set and when? Who was the king and why had he given the order for all male children under the age of two to be killed?

Clues

1 The king was visited and not visited by three wise men before this happened.

2 This happened in the same town in which Jesus was born.

3 The fact that the king only ordered the killing of male children is significant.

Riddles From Classical Music

Over 25 well-known scenes from the world of classical music presented as riddles suitable for use with Odyssey boards. Each riddle is presented with an enticing title, a set of clues, a detailed historical essay outlining the facts and context in which the events take place, and a list of cross-curricula activities that could lead out from an exploration of the subject.

Ouch!

A handsome man, dressed in a long velvet frock coat, with silk embroidery, over tunic and breeches, stockinged legs and shoes that matched his coat, ornamented with silver buckles, is standing in front of an orchestra in the hall of mirrors at Versailles, in a long flowing wig of curls. He's conducting a small orchestra of superb musicians – the best in the country in a piece of music he's composed to celebrate his patron's recovery from illness. In his mind, he's conducting a ritual. He's recreating and rebalancing the music of the spheres, for he sees himself as one of the satellites which revolve around their patron, their central sun. He beats time using a device like a long walking stick. At a particularly dramatic cadence, he accidentally hits his foot. It's painful, but he doesn't cry out.

Who is this man? Who is his patron? Where are they and when? What happens to the conductor as a result and why?

Clues

1 The musician started out as a dancer and loved composing ballets for his patron, who particularly enjoyed dancing.
2 The musician is credited with the invention of the French style of opera known as Lyric Tragedy (Tragédie Lyrique).
3 The musician was the friend of the French playwright, Molière, with whom he collaborated on several occasions.

4 The patron was known as The Sun King.
5 The patron was the fourteenth person to adopt the name of
  Louis.

Further titles in the Treasure Trove Series of Cultural Riddles

Riddles From Myths and Legends
Riddles From Children's Literature
Riddles From Literature
Maths Riddles
Riddles From Popular Music
Riddles From Science
Riddles From Architecture
Riddles From Geography
Riddles From The World of the Moving Image

Notes

1   Pirsig (2004), page 178.

2   *Educare* (2008), page 34.

3   See www.odysseygrids.com.

4   See pages 186–194 and www.odysseygrids.com.

5   ... *the 'instruction model' of teaching... [in which] the child is the empty mug, the teacher is the full jug, the jug is tipped into the empty mug – hey presto, education has happened.* Michael Rosen, in Tims (2010), page 9.

6   See Santarcangeli (2000), pages 37–56.

7   See Ruskin (1895), pages 107–133.

8   See Marzano, Pickering and Pollock (2001).

9   Haven (2007), page 104.

10 Lahad (1992); Lahad and Ayalon (1993), pages 117–145.

11 For a documented example of this flexible use of form from outside the context of performance storytelling, where it is common practice, see Dent-Brown (1999).

12 Jacobs (1890), pages 59–67.

13 Csíkszentmihályi (2002).

14 Gray, Brown and Macanufo (2010).

15 See suggestions in the Resources Section in the Bibliography, on pages 178–180.

16 See www.odysseygrids.com.

17 See pages 186–194 and www.odysseygrids.com.

18 See www.odysseygrids.com.

19 Kagan Structures referred to in this work are cited with permission from Kagan Publishing and Professional Development from Kagan, Kagan and Kagan, *Classbuilding: Cooperative Learning Structures* (2012); Kagan and Kagan, *Cooperative Learning* (2009); Kagan, Kyle and Scott, *Win-Win Discipline* (2004); Michels, *Cooperative Learning and Science* (2003) and Kagan and Kagan, *Teambuilding* (2001).

www.KaganOnline.com.

20   Kagan and Kagan (2009), Chapter 12. This is a compressed mnemonic version of Johnson and Johnson's five principles (1984), as outlined in the Foundation Coalition's publication, *Positive Interdependence, Individual Accountability, Promotive Interaction: Three Pillars of Cooperative Learning* (no date).

21   Kagan and Kagan (2009), page xii.

21a The details of the steps of these Kagan Structures can be found in Kagan and Kagan (2009), pages 6.25–6.38.

21b The details of the steps of these Kagan Structures can be found in Kagan and Kagan (2009), pages 6.32–6.38, 12.6.

22   Panitz (1996).

23   Dolci (1973), page 146.

24   Grove and Panzer (1989).

25   For use in therapy, see Grove and Panzer (1989); Lawley and Tompkins (2000); Sullivan and Rees (2008); and Harland (2012), among others; for use in education, see Walker (TEDx Merseyside talk, 4 February 2012), Walker (Podcast, February 2012), McCracken (Podcast, April 2012); for use in corporate training, see Walker (DVD).

26   See McCracken (2013).

27   Stahl (1994).

28   Inspired by an exercise in Win Wenger's *You are Brighter than You Think!*, page 3 number 24, published on line at www.winwenger.com/ebooks/bright3.htm.

29   Magic Floating Cube – Optical Illusion www.youtube.com/watch?v=FlO7zCV0Ctg.

30   See www.odysseygrids.com.

31   Boyer (1991), page 229.

32   Kagan and Kagan (2009), page 14.7.

33   See, for instance, the Mathematics Enhancement Program GSCE resource on the Centre for Innovation in Mathematics Teaching Website, Unit 10.5 – www.cimt.plymouth.ac.uk/projects/mepres/allgcse/pr10-sa.pdf, or one of the

websites listed in the Resources Section on pages 178–180.

34 Kagan and Kagan (2009), page 14.7.

35 Sanzi Jing, *Three-Character Classic* – on-line version at the Yellow Bridge website – www.yellowbridge.com/onlinelit/ sanzijing.php.

36 Quoted in Norbu (1989), page 48.

37 Kagan and Kagan (2009), page 14.7.

38 Kagan and Kagan (2009), page 14.7.

39 Kagan and Kagan (2009), page 14.7.

40 Kagan and Kagan (2009), page 14.7.

41 Turner (2006), page 12.

42 Vygotsky (1999), page 244.

43 See, for instance, the Mathematics Enhancement Program resource on the Centre for Innovation in Mathematics Teaching Website, Book 9, Unit 11.1 – www.cimt .plymouth.ac.uk/projects/mepres/book9/bk9i11/bk9_11i1.ht ml, or one of the websites listed in the Resources Section on pages 178–180.

44 de Bono (1967).

45 de Bono (1982/95), pages 18–24.

46 Kagan and Kagan (2009), page 14.7.

47 See, for instance, the Mathematics Enhancement Program resource on the Centre for Innovation in Mathematics Teaching Website, GCSE book, Unit 10.4 – www.cimt. plymouth.ac.uk/projects/mepres/allgcse/pr10-sa.pdf, or one of the websites listed in the Resources Section on pages 178–80.

48 Kagan and Kagan (2009), page 14.7.

49 Hyde, CR, *Pay It Forward*, Simon and Schuster, New York, 1999.

50 Kagan and Kagan (2009), page 14.7.

51 www.armagetronad.org

52 See, for instance, the Mathematics Enhancement Program resource on the Centre for Innovation in Mathematics

Teaching Website, Book 8, Unit 12.1 – www.cimt. plymouth.ac.uk/projects/mepres/book8/bk8_12.pdf, or one of the websites listed in the Resources Section on pages 178–180.

53 See, for instance, the Mathematics Enhancement Program resource on the Centre for Innovation in Mathematics Teaching Website, Book 7, Unit 16.3 – www.cimt. plymouth.ac.uk/projects/mepres/book7/bk7_16.pdf, or one of the websites listed in the Resources Section on pages 178–80.

54 Kagan and Kagan (2009), page 14.7.

55 www.ecosquared.info.

56 Wilhelm/Baynes (1997), page 322. (I've translated 'wording' for 'words' to differentiate it from text; Chinese speakers never think they are 'speaking characters' – DP.)

57 Kagan and Kagan (2009), page 14.7.

Liberalis is a Latin word which evokes ideas of freedom, liberality, generosity of spirit, dignity, honour, books, the liberal arts education tradition and the work of the Greek grammarian and storyteller Antonius Liberalis. We seek to combine all these interlinked aspects in the books we publish.

We bring classical ways of thinking and learning in touch with traditional storytelling and the latest thinking in terms of educational research and pedagogy in an approach that combines the best of the old with the best of the new.

As classical education publishers, our books are designed to appeal to readers across the globe who are interested in expanding their minds in the quest of knowledge. We cater for primary, secondary and higher education markets, homeschoolers, parents and members of the general public who have a love of ongoing learning.

If you have a proposal that you think would be of interest to Liberalis, submit your inquiry in the first instance via the website: www.liberalisbooks.com.